# CHONDOGYO SCRIPTURE

*Donggyeong Daejeon*
(Great Scripture of Eastern Learning)

Translated by
**Yong Choon Kim**
and
**Suk San Yoon**
with
**Central Headquarters of Chondogyo**

University Press of America,® Inc.
Lanham · Boulder · New York · Toronto · Plymouth, UK

Copyright © 2007 by
University Press of America,® Inc.
4501 Forbes Boulevard
Suite 200
Lanham, Maryland 20706
UPA Acquisitions Department (301) 459-3366

Published with the support of the Korea Literature Translation Institute

Estover Road
Plymouth PL6 7PY
United Kingdom

All rights reserved
Printed in the United States of America
British Library Cataloging in Publication Information Available

Library of Congress Control Number: 2007932049
ISBN-13: 978-0-7618-3802-9 (paperback : alk. paper)
ISBN-10: 0-7618-3802-3 (paperback : alk. paper)

∞™ The paper used in this publication meets the minimum
requirements of American National Standard for Information
Sciences—Permanence of Paper for Printed Library Materials,
ANSI Z39.48—1984

# CONTENTS

PREFACE ........................................................................................... v
CHONDOGYO SCRIPTURE ............................................................. 1
    ON PROPAGATING TRUTH (*PODEOK-MUN*) ........................... 3
    A DISCUSSION ON LEARNING (*NONHAK-MUN*) ..................... 7
    ON CULTIVATING VIRTUE (*SUDEOK-MUN*) .......................... 15
    NOT SO, YET SO (*BURYEON GIYEON*) ................................... 21
    POEMS, INCANTATIONS, AND OTHER WRITINGS ................ 25
        *ON BLESSING* ........................................................................ 25
        *INCANTATION* ...................................................................... 26
        *POEM ON THE ARRIVAL OF SPRING* .................................. 28
        *ON DESTINY* ......................................................................... 29
        *THE POEM I RECEIVED FROM GOD* ................................... 30
        *PROVERBS* ............................................................................ 31
        *POEM IN RESPONSE TO GOD'S TEACHING* ....................... 32
        *LAMENTING THE HASTY MIND OF THE DISCIPLES* ....... 36
        *WORDS ACCORDING TO DIVINE WILL* ............................. 38
        *COLLECTION OF WORDS* .................................................... 39
        *THE FIRST EIGHT VERSES* ................................................. 42
        *THE SECOND EIGHT VERSES* ............................................ 44
        *WRITING ON THEME* ........................................................... 46
        *THE SONG THAT WE SING AT NIGHT* ............................... 47
        *THE WAY OF WRITING* ....................................................... 50
        *SONG ON HIGH AND FLOW* ............................................... 51
        *POEM WITH A SUDDEN REALIZATION* ............................ 52

## Contents

*OTHER POEMS* ............................................................................ *53*
APPENDIX A. CHONDOGYO: WHAT KIND OF RELIGION IS IT? ........ 55
    HISTORY OF CHONDOGYO .................................................... 55
    UNDERSTANDING CHONDOGYO SCRIPTURE ................................ 62
APPENDIX B. IMPORTANT TERMS AND IDEAS OF CHONDOGYO .... 65
    *Jigi* (The Ultimate Energy) ......................................................... 65
    *Si Cheonju* (Bearing/Serving God Within Me) ............................... 66
    *Susim Jeonggi* (Keeping the Pure Mind and Having Right Conduct) ......... 67
    *Muwi Ihwa* (Natural Becoming) ................................................. 70
    *Buryeon Giyeon* (Not So, Yet So) ............................................... 71
    *Donggwi Ilche* (Returning to the Origin and Becoming One) ............... 74
ENDNOTES .............................................................................. 77
GLOSSARY .............................................................................. 87

# PREFACE

Chondogyo, which means The Religion of the Heavenly Way, was founded in Korea by Suun Choe Je-u in 1860. It was originally called Donghak, which means Eastern Learning. Many scholars, familiar with Korean religions, philosophies and history, acknowledge Donghak/Chondogyo as the most important new religion of Korea. They recognize the significant contributions that Donghak/Chondogyo made in modern Korean history.

Korea was not well known in the Western world until the Korean War of 1950. Since then, Korea has gradually become known as a country with a long history and a unique culture. The rapid growth of the economy in recent years has contributed to the recognition of Korea as a dynamic, modern nation.

In the last several decades, Western scholarship on Korea has been growing gradually. An increasing number of books on Korean studies have been published in the Western languages, however, books on Korean religions and philosophies are still relatively small in number. Books on Donghak/Chondogyo are especially few.

I wrote my PhD dissertation on *The Concept of Man in Chondogyo* in 1969. Several years later the revised version of it was published as *The Chondogyo Concept of Man*. My co-translator, Dr. Suk-san Yoon published a book in 2002 entitled *Chondogyo: The Religion of Cosmos That Blossomed in Korea* which was later translated into English.

In most religions, scripture plays one of the key roles in beliefs and practices. My translations of parts of Donghak/Chondogyo scripture were published in *Sourcebook of Korean Civilization,* Vol. 2 (1996) and in *Sources of Korean Tradition,* Vol. 2 (2000), both published by Columbia University Press.

## Preface

This book contains a complete translation of *Donggyeong Daejeon* (The Great Scripture of Eastern Learning), which is the main part of Chondogyo Scripture. *Donggyeong Daejeon* was written in *Hanmun* (Chinese characters with Korean pronunciation). The other part of the Chondogyo Scripture is *Yongdam Yusa* (The Songs of Yongdam), which was written in *Han-geul* (Korean script). A detailed introduction of Chondogyo and its Scripture is added in the Appendices.

Appendix B was written by Dr. Yoon and was translated by me into English, with additional notes for the interpretation and clarification of some difficult points. I have used the new Romanization system that was developed in 2000 by the Ministry of Culture and Tourism of the Korean government for terms in Korean.

Dr. Yoon and I have been working on this translation project for a long time. We deeply appreciate the superb editorial help provided by Dr. Kirsten Bell, an anthropology professor at Macquarie University in Australia, who wrote a PhD dissertation on Chondogyo. We also greatly appreciate the skillful editorial and layout assistance provided by Mr. James Walton, a longtime resident of Korea and friend of Dr. Yoon. We are very grateful for the translation grants provided by the Korean Literature Translation Institute and the Central Headquarters of Chondogyo.

Yong Choon Kim<br>
University of Rhode Island<br>
Kingston, R.I.<br>
U.S.A.<br>
March 2006

*Front cover photo*: Chondogyo Scripture: Original Chondogyo Cononical Writings: Left: A woodblock print in Chinese from Donghak Scripture. Right: A woodblock print in Korean Hangeul script from the Songs of Yongdam. After 1860 Suun, Choe Je-U wrote many pieces in order to teach his followers concerning important ideas and doctrines of Donghak/Chondogyo. He produced three kinds of writing. The first type consists of somewhat long pieces written in Chinese to descript the essential ideas and truth of Donghak. They include Podeok-mun.

*Back cover photo (left)*: The Birthplace of Chondogyo: This is where Suun was met by Hanullim (God) and received his talisman and the instructions to take his message to the world.

*Back cover photo (right)*: Chondogyo Founder Great Master Suun Choe Je-U.

# CHONDOGYO SCRIPTURE

## *DONGGYEONG DAEJEON* (東經大全 GREAT SCRIPTURE OF EASTERN LEARNING)

**Chondogyo Symbol of Gung-Eul**

This symbol is based on the talisman that Suun received from *Hanullim* (God), when he had his religious experience in April 1860

# ON PROPAGATING TRUTH
(布德文 *PODEOK-MUN*)[1]

1. 盖自上古以來 春秋迭代 四時盛衰 不遷不易 是亦 天主造化之迹 昭然于天下也

Since the beginning of time, the four seasons of spring, summer, autumn, and winter have rotated in an orderly way. When spring runs its course, summer comes; when summer runs its course, autumn arrives; when autumn runs its course, winter arrives. The exchanges of seasons have been repeating in an orderly fashion without error since the beginning of the world. The natural environment, in which humankind and all beings live, has been shaped according to the changes of seasons. This order of seasons, the order of nature, is evidence of the power of God,[2] *Hanullim*, by which all things are made.[3]

2. 愚夫愚民 未知雨露之澤 知其無爲而化矣

However, the ignorant people of the world did not know that God sent rain and dew, by which all things were renewed and grew. They thought that all things began and developed naturally.

3. 自五帝之後 聖人以生 日月星辰 天地度數 成出文券 而以定天道之常然 一動一靜 一盛一敗 付之於天命 是敬天命 而順天理者也 故 人成君子 學成道德 道則天道 德則天德 明其道而修其德 故 乃成君子 至於至聖 豈不欽歎哉

In ancient China, there were five virtuous kings, who made wise laws and ruled the people with compassion and justice. Thereafter, sages were born and they determined the movements of the sun, moon, and stars, and they made a calendar and a book of astronomy. Then, they determined the unchanging nature of the Heavenly Way.[4] They taught that the mind and actions of humankind as well as all the changes of the universe depended on the Will of Heaven.[5] The sages had reverence for the Will of Heaven and followed the Principle of Heaven.[6]

The people who respected the Will of Heaven and followed the Principle of Heaven became superior men,[7] and through their learning they attained a high level of moral virtue. The way that they followed is called the Heavenly Way and the virtue that they cultivated is called the Heavenly Virtue.[8] Having been enlightened by the Heavenly Way and having cultivated Virtue, the people of ancient times became superior men and, furthermore, some of them became great sages. Isn't it a wonderful and joyful event?!!

4. 又此挽近以來 一世之人 各自爲心 不順天理 不顧天命 心常悚然 莫知所向矣

However, in current times the people of the world have selfish minds, and do not follow the Principle of Heaven nor care for the Will of Heaven. Therefore, my mind is always anxious and fearful, and I don't know what will happen in the future.

5. 至於庚申 傳聞西洋之人 以爲天主之意 不取富貴 攻取天下 立其堂 行其道 故吾亦有其然豈其然之疑

In 1860 there were rumors that in order to serve God's will, the Westerners were not seeking wealth or glory, yet they attacked and conquered the world, and built their churches and spread their religion.[9] I also wonder whether it was true and why they did that.

6. 不意四月 心寒身戰 疾不得執症 言不得難狀之際 有何仙語 忽入耳中 驚起探問則 曰勿懼勿恐 世人謂我上帝 汝不知上帝耶 問其所然 曰余亦無功 故生汝世間 敎人此法 勿疑勿疑 曰然則西道以敎人乎 曰不然 吾有靈符 其名僊藥 其形太極 又形弓弓 受我此符 濟人疾病 受我呪文 敎人爲我則 汝亦長生 布德天下矣

Unexpectedly, in April, my mind felt chilled and my body shook. I felt ill but did not know exactly what was wrong and I could not describe the condition of my feeling. Then, suddenly, a mysterious voice came to my ear, and I was frightened and woke up and asked, "Who are you?"[10]

The voice said: "Do not fear and do not be afraid. Humankind calls me *Sangje* (God); don't you recognize *Sangje*?"[11]

I asked, "Why do you reveal yourself to me?" God said: "I have not been able to find anyone to teach the Truth. Thus, I am sending you to the world to teach the Truth. Therefore, do not ever doubt it."

I asked God, "Shall I teach the Western (Christian) truth?" God said, "No. I have a talisman (spiritual symbol) which is called mystical medicine.[12] Its shape is like the Great Ultimate[13] and its form is also like *gung gung*.[14] Receive this talisman and cure humankind's illness.[15] Receive also my incantation[16] and teach people to honor me. Then, you too shall become immortal and the Truth shall spread to all the world."

7. 吾亦感其言 受其符 書以吞服 則潤身差病 方乃知仙藥矣 到此 用病則 或有差不差 故莫知其端 察其所然則 誠之又誠 至爲天主者 每每有中 不順道德者 一一無驗 此非受人之誠敬耶

Deeply moved by the words of God, I took the talisman, drew it on a piece of paper and swallowed it.[17] Then suddenly I felt healthy and my illness vanished, and I realized that the mystical medicine was responsible. When I applied it to the illnesses of other people, some were cured but others were not. Not knowing the exact reason for this, I watched carefully and discovered that sincere and true believers who honored God got positive results, and those who disobeyed the Truth and disregarded Virtue had no good result at all. Therefore, isn't it all based on the sincerity and reverence of the recipient?

8. 是故 我國惡疾滿世 民無四時之安 是亦傷害之數也 西洋戰勝 攻取 無事不成 而天下盡滅 亦不無脣亡之歎 輔國安民 計將安出

Recently, our country has been filled with evil things.[18] The people live in a time without peace. This is an indication of the bad fortune of our nation.

The Western powers are victorious whenever they fight, and they succeed and takeover wherever they attack. There seems to be nothing that they cannot achieve. I am worried that if China is destroyed, Korea may be next.[19] Where can we find a way for supporting the nation and comforting the people?[20]

9. 惜哉 於今世人 未知時運 聞我斯言則 入則心非 出則巷議 不順
道德 甚可畏也 賢者聞之 其或不然 而吾將慨歎 世則無奈 忘略記出
諭以示之 敬受此書 欽哉訓辭

  Alas! The people of this generation do not understand that a new age is coming.[21] After listening to my words, they go home and deny them in their minds, and when they are outside their house, they gossip about my teaching. Thus, they do not follow Truth and Virtue.[22] This is truly a worrisome situation.

  The wise men hear the gossip and reject it as false. It is regrettable that I cannot convince everyone in the world. I am writing this (*Podeok-mun*) to instruct the people. Receive this writing with respect and admire my teaching always.

# A DISCUSSION ON LEARNING
# (論學文 *NONHAK-MUN*)[23]

1. 夫天道者 如無形而有迹 地理者 如廣大而有方者也 故天有 九星 以應九州 地有八方 以應八卦 而有盈虛迭代之數 無動靜變易之理 陰陽相均 雖百千萬物 化出於其中 獨惟人最靈者也

    The Heavenly Way is formless but has traces.[24] The earth is vast and great, yet it has directions. Heaven has the nine stars,[25] and likewise the earth has the nine provinces.[26] The earth also has eight directions which correspond to the eight trigrams[27] of humankind. All things and all changes in the universe are interpreted according to the eight trigrams. Thus, the universe consists of numbers and principles according to which waxing and waning are exchanged, and movement and quietness are rotated without mistake or change.[28]

    Among the myriad things in the universe which are produced through the interplay of *yin* and *yang*,[29] humans alone are the most spiritual beings.

2. 故定三才之理 出五行之數 五行者 何也 天爲五行之綱 地爲五行之質 人爲五行之氣 天地人三才之數 於斯可見矣

    Thus, the principle of three essentials (of Heaven, earth, and human beings) is established, and the number of the five agents was produced.[30] What are the relations of the five agents? Heaven is the principle of the five agents, the earth is the basis of the five agents, and humankind is the vital force of the five agents. Therefore, we can understand that Heaven, earth, and humans constitute the essentials of the universe.

3. 四時盛衰 風露霜雪 不失其時 不變其序 如露蒼生 莫知其端 或云天主之恩 或云化工之迹 然而以恩言之 惟爲不見之事 以工言之 亦爲難狀之言 何者 於古及今 其中未必者也

The four seasons rotate without a change of order, and wind, dew, frost, and snow appear in a timely manner. Many people, who are like dew, do not understand the reasons for it. Some people say that it is God's grace, and others say that it is the work of nature. However, even though some people say that it is the grace of God, it cannot be shown, and even though others say that it is the work of nature, it is difficult to prove. Thus, from the ancient times to the present time, people do not know exactly the real reason for it.[31]

4. 夫庚申之年 建巳之月 天下紛亂 民心淆薄 莫知所向之地 又有怪違之說 崩騰于世間 西洋之人 道成立德 及其造化 無事不成 攻鬪干戈 無人在前 中國消滅 豈可無脣亡之患耶 都緣無他 斯人道稱西道 學稱天主 敎則聖敎 此非知天時 而受天命耶

In April 1860 the country was in chaos, and the minds of the people were confused, and no direction or solution was known. Strange rumors were rampant in the country: the Westerners have realized Truth and Virtue, and through their inventions they can accomplish anything, and if they attack with their weapons, no one can withstand them. If China is destroyed, wouldn't Korea face the same fate?[32] Is the reason for their success none other than the way that they call the Western way: the learning that they call Catholicism and the religion that they call holy religion? Do they know perhaps the time of Heaven and did they receive the mandate of Heaven?[33]

5. 擧此一一不已故 吾亦悚然 只有恨生晚之際 身多戰寒 外有接靈之氣 內有降話之敎 視之不見 聽之不聞 心尙怪訝 修心正氣而問曰 何爲若然也

When I consider each of these questions, I have a feeling of anxiety and regret that I was born at this late time. Around this time, suddenly my body shook, I felt a chill and I felt the vital force of contact with the Spirit, and inwardly I heard divine words of instruction. I looked around but could not see anyone. I listened but could not hear anything. Therefore, I felt it very strange.[34] After bracing my mind and renewing my energy, I asked, "Why is it like this?"

6. 曰吾心卽汝心也 人何知之 知天地而無知鬼神 鬼神者 吾也 及汝无窮无窮之道 修而煉之 制其文敎人 定其法布德 則令汝長生 昭然于天下矣

The divine answer was, "My mind is your mind.³⁵ How can humankind know it? People know of Heaven and earth, but they do not know the Spirit. I am the Spirit.³⁶ As I am giving you the eternal Truth, cultivate and refine it, write it down and teach it to the people. Establish the laws of practice and propagate the Truth (virtue). Then you will have eternal life and will brighten the world."

7. 吾亦幾至一歲 修而度之 則亦不無自然之理 故一以作呪文 一以作降靈之法 一以作不忘之詞 次第道法 猶爲二十一字而已

For almost a year I practiced and contemplated the Way, and then I realized that it is none other than the Principle of Nature.³⁷ Therefore, once I composed the incantations, I created the technique for receiving the Divine Spirit, and then I wrote a poem of "Not forgetting God."³⁸ I realized that the orderly technique of practicing the Way lies only in the twenty-one character incantation.³⁹

8. 轉至辛酉 四方賢士 進我而問曰 今天靈 降臨先生 何爲其然也 曰受其无往不復之理也 曰然則何道以名之 曰天道也 曰與洋道 無異者乎 曰洋學 如斯而有異 如呪而無實 然而 運則一也 道則同也 理則非也

In the following year, 1861, intelligent scholars from every place came to me and asked, "(We heard that) the Heavenly Spirit descended upon you; what happened?" I replied, "I received the principle of Nature, which repeats in coming and going." They asked, "What is name of your way?" I replied, "It is the Heavenly Way." They asked, "What is the difference from the Western Way?" I answered, "The Western religion (Christianity) is similar but different. It has the appearance of worshiping God, but has no substance. They both have the same destiny as religions and their Way (Truth) is identical, but their doctrines are different."⁴⁰

9. 曰何爲其然也 曰吾道无爲而化矣 守其心定其氣 率其性受其敎 化出於自然之中 西人 言無次第 書無皂白而頓無爲天主之端 只祝自爲身之謀 身無氣化之神 學无天主之敎 有形無迹 如思无呪 道近虛無 學非天主 豈可謂无異者乎

They asked, "Why is that so?" I answered, "Our Way is the Natural Way.[41] If each person preserves a good mind, rectifies the vital force, follows their original nature, and receives the Divine teaching, all will turn out well naturally. The Westerners have no order in their words and no logic in their writings. There is no genuine service for God but they only pray for selfish ideas. Therefore, they do not have the mystical experience of uniting with the spiritual force, and they lack the true teaching of God. Their religion has form but no substance. They have vague ideas but no real incantation. Their religion is close to emptiness and their theology is not really for God. Therefore, how can one say that there is no difference between the Western religion and my teaching?

10. 曰同道言之 則名其西學也 曰不然 吾亦生於東 受於東 道雖天道 學則東學 況地分東西 西何謂東 東何謂西 孔子生於鄒風於鄒 鄒魯之風 傳遺於斯世 吾道受於斯 布於斯 豈可謂以西名之者乎

They asked, "You said that the Way is identical; then, could you call your Way Western Learning?" I replied, "No, I was born in the East, and I received it in the East. Therefore, although the Way is called the Heavenly Way,[42] the learning is called *Donghak* (Eastern Learning). As the world is divided between the east and west, how can the west be called the east, and the east be called the west? Confucius was born in the state of Lu and taught in Tsou. Therefore, his teaching is called the school of Tsou-Lu and spread throughout the world. Likewise, I received the Way in this land (Korea) and spread it here. Therefore, how can it be called Western Learning?"

11. 曰呪文之意 何也 曰至爲天主之字故 以呪言之 今文有古文有

They asked, "What is the meaning of the incantation?" I answered, "The incantation is words which honor God with the utmost sincerity. There are incantations today as there were incantations in the ancient times.[43]

12. 曰降靈之文 何爲其然也 曰至者 極焉之爲 至氣者 虛靈蒼蒼 無事不涉 無事不命 然而 如形而難狀 如聞而難見 是亦渾元之一氣也 今至者 於斯入道 知其氣接者也 願爲者 請祝之意也 大降者 氣化之願也

They asked, "What is the meaning of the incantation which prays for the descent of the Spirit?" I answered: "The ultimate (*ji*) means the highest and extremely great.[44] The vital force(*ji-ki*)[45] is like the mysterious Spirit, and it is vast and full in the universe. It touches and governs all things. It looks like it has a form, but it is difficult to describe. It seems to have sound, yet it is difficult to understand. It is the one Ultimate Energy of the vast universe. *Geum-ji* (今至) means that now one joins the church (Donghak/Chondogyo) and understands the meaning of uniting with the vital force (of God). *Weon-wi* (願爲) means hoping and praying. *Dae-gang* (大降) means uniting with the Ultimate Energy."

13. 侍者 內有神靈 外有氣化 一世之人 各知不移者也 主者 稱其尊而與父母同事者也 造化者 無爲而化也 定者 合其德 定其心也 永世者 人之平生也 不忘者 存想之意也 萬事者 數之多也 知者 知其道而受其知也 故明明其德 念念不忘 則至化至氣 至於至聖

$Si^{46}$ means having the Divine Spirit within and expressing the vital force in life. When people realize this they will keep it in their hearts without change. $Ju^{47}$ refers to respecting, honoring, and serving God like one's own parents. *Johwa*$^{48}$ means natural becoming and transformation. *Jeong*$^{49}$ means oneness with the Divine Virtue and deciding to have the mind of God. *Yeongse*$^{50}$ refers to the long life of humankind. *Bulmang*$^{51}$ means thinking about God always without forgetting. *Mansa*$^{52}$ means many things. $Ji^{53}$ means understanding God's way and achieving wisdom. Thus, if one would think about and never forget the bright Truth and Virtue of God and the incantation, one will unite with the Ultimate Energy (*ji-gi*) of God and attain the perfect sagehood.

14. 曰天心卽人心 則何有善惡也 曰命其人貴賤之殊 定其人苦樂之理 然而君子之德 氣有正而心有定 故與天地合其德 小人之德 氣不正而心有移 故與天地違其命 此非盛衰之理耶

The disciples asked, "If the mind of God is identical with the mind of humans,$^{54}$ why is there good and evil?" I answered: "God ordains the standard of high and low qualities of life, and God determines the principle of joy and sorrow. The virtues of the superior man$^{55}$ consist of right energy (vital force)$^{56}$ and a stable mind and, therefore, his virtue is one with the virtue of the universe. However, the inferior man has wrong energy and an unstable mind and therefore violates the will of God. Isn't this the principle of success (good) and failure (evil)?"$^{57}$

15. 曰一世之人 何不敬天主也 曰臨死號天 人之常情 而命乃在天 天生萬民 古之聖人之 所謂而尙今彌留 然而似然非然之間 未知詳然之故也

The disciples asked, "Why don't the peoples of the world revere God?" I answered: "To call out to God when they are facing death is the common inclination of all humans. The ancient sages said that the destiny of human beings is determined by God's will and that God produced all humankind. Such sayings remain valid even today. However, the peoples of the world do not revere God, because they do not know exactly whether God exists or not.

16. 曰毀道者 何也 曰猶或可也 曰何以可也 曰吾道 今不聞古不聞之事 今不比古不比之法也 修者 如虛而有實 聞者 如實而有虛也

The disciples asked, "Why do some people disparage your teaching?" I answered, "Sometimes it can happen." They asked, "How is it possible?" I replied: "Because my Way is the Truth which no one has heard in the past until now, and it is incomparable to anything in the present or in the past.[58] Cultivating and practicing my Way may appear to be futile but has a real and positive result, while merely listening is futile, although it may have the appearance of some result.[59]

17. 曰反道而歸者 何也 曰斯人者 不足擧論也 曰胡不擧論也 曰敬而遠之 曰前何心而後何心也 曰草上之風也 曰然則何以降靈也 曰不擇善惡也 曰無害無德也 曰堯舜之世 民皆爲堯舜 斯世之運 與世同歸 有害有德 在於天主 不在於我也 一一究心 則害及其身 未詳知之 然而斯人享福 不可使聞於他人 非君之所問也 非我之所關也

The disciples asked, "Why do some people betray your Way and turn away from it?" I answered, "It is not even worth discussing them." They asked, "Why it is not worth talking about them?" I answered: "By distancing from them, you avoid harm." They asked, "What was in their minds when they came in and what was in their minds when they left?" I answered: "Their minds are shaky like grass over which the wind blows." They asked, "Then, how can those people receive the Spirit?" I answered: "God's Spirit is given whether they are good or bad."[60] They asked, "Isn't there good fortune and misfortune?"[61] I replied: "At the time of the reign of the benevolent kings, Yao and Shun, the people were good like Yao and Shun.[62] The destiny of this world is moving toward the same direction. The good fortunes and misfortunes are in the hands of God and not in my power. As we investigate each one, we do not know clearly whether they will have misfortune, and we cannot tell whether they will enjoy good fortune, for good fortune and misfortune are neither what you should ask for nor my business to ask for.

18. 嗚呼噫噫 諸君之問道 何若是明明也 雖我拙文 未及於精義正

宗 然而矯其人修其身 養其才正其心 豈可有岐貳之端乎 凡天地无窮之數 道之無極之理 皆載此書 惟我諸君 敬受此書 以助聖德 於我比之 則況若甘受和白受采 吾今樂道 不勝欽歎故 論而言之 諭而示之 明而察之 不失玄機

Wow! Amazing! How brilliant are your questions about the Way! My rough writings may not fully convey the deep meaning of the Truth, but how can there be any doubt that it can correct people, cultivate human conduct, develop human potential, and restore a right mind!

The infinite Truth of Heaven and earth and the ultimate principle of the Way are all contained in this writing. Receive this writing respectfully and help to spread the holy Truth of God. If I could compare this, it is like a harmony of taste made by sweetness and colors absorbed by whiteness. Now I enjoy the Way and my joy is overwhelming! Thus, I am teaching and showing this Truth to you. Study it carefully and clearly, and never lose the profound opportunity provided by God.

# ON CULTIVATING VIRTUE
(修德文 *SUDEOK-MUN*)⁶³

1. 元亨利貞 天道之常 惟一執中 人事之察 故生而知之 夫子之聖質 學而知之 先儒之相傳 雖有困而得之 淺見薄識 皆由於吾師之盛德 不失於先王之古禮

To give birth to all things, to grow them, to let them bear fruit, and to harvest them is the constant Way of Heaven.⁶⁴ To obey and follow the constant Way of Heaven with a single mindedness is the proper conduct of humankind. To know all this from birth was Confucius' sagely native understanding. To know this by learning was the tradition of the former scholars. Although shallow and insignificant, the knowledge that people gain through study comes from the virtuous teachings of the former scholars, and they follow the propriety of ancient kings.⁶⁵

2. 余出自東方 無了度日 僅保家聲 未免寒士 先祖之忠義 節有餘於龍山 吾王之盛德 歲復回於壬丙 若是餘蔭 不絕如流 家君出世 名盖一道 無不士林之共知 德承六世 豈非子孫之餘慶

Having been born in the East, I was spending each day without meaningful work, barely preserving my family name and unable to escape the condition of a poor scholar. My ancestors' loyalty and uprightness left their mark in Yongsan.⁶⁶ In accordance with the great virtue of our king, the year of *imjin* and the year of *byeongja* return.⁶⁷ The virtue of my ancestors flowed down without interruption, and after my father was born, his name was known throughout the province, and there was no scholar who did not know his name. This fame has continued for six generations; isn't it a glory for the descendants?

3. 噫 學士之平生 光陰之春夢 年至四十 工知芭籬之邊物 心無青雲之大道 一以作歸去來之辭 一以詠覺非是之句 携筇理履 況若處士之行 山高水長 莫非先生之風 龜尾之奇峯怪石 月城金鰲之北 龍湫之淸潭寶溪 古都馬龍之西 園中桃花 恐知漁子之舟 屋前滄波 意在太公之釣 檻臨池塘 無違濂溪之志 亭號龍潭 豈非慕葛之心

    Alas! My father's life as a scholar was like a transient spring dream. He studied until he was forty, but his knowledge was useless and he had no desire to become a government official. He composed a song about returning home from a government position, realizing that rural life is ideal.[68] Carrying a bamboo cane and wearing wooden clogs, he looked like the reclusive scholar Tao Yuan-Ming of ancient China. His character was lofty and steady like a high mountain and long river, and thus he resembled Yen Tzu-ling.[69]

    Gumi Mountain, which has wondrous peaks and mysterious rocks, lies to the north of Weolseong and Geumo Mountain.[70] The clear pond and the beautiful stream of Yongchu[71] are west of Maryong[72] in the ancient city of Gyeongju. I am wondering whether fishermen will find this beautiful peach flower garden.[73] The beautiful water flowing in front of the house is like the place where Chiang T'ai-kung's mind would have been.[74] The deck of the pavilion near the lotus flower pond reflects the will of Chou Tun-i.[75] The pavilion was named Yongdam, as it admires the mind of Chuke Liang.[76]

4. 難禁歲月之如流 哀臨一日化仙 孤我一命 年至二八 何以知之 無異童子 先考平生之事業 無痕於火中 子孫不肖之餘恨 落心於世間 豈不痛哉 豈不惜哉

    As the flow of time cannot be stopped, one day my father passed away, and I experienced deep sorrow. I was left alone at the age of sixteen. What could I know, since I was not very different from a child. As the life work of my father perished in a fire without a trace, I grieved about my lack of ability as his descendant and lost hope in this world. Isn't this a mournful and sorrowful thing!?

5. 心有家庭之業 安知稼穡之役 書無工課之篤 意墮靑雲之志 家産漸衰 未知末梢之如何 年光漸盆 可歎身勢之將拙 料難八字 又有寒飢之慮 念來四十 豈無不成之歎 巢穴未定 誰云天地之廣大 所業交違 自憐一身之難藏 自是由來 擺脫世間之扮撓 賣去胸海之硼結

I wanted to work and support my family, but I did not know farming. Since I did not study the classics deeply, I could not hope for a government position. As the assets of my family had gradually decreased, I did not know what might happen in the future. As I grew older, I lamented the decline in the condition of my life. As I contemplated my destiny, I feared the possibility of coldness and hunger. As I contemplated the approaching age of forty, how could I not lament my lack of success in life? As I did not have a definite place to live, who could say that Heaven and earth are wide and big? As all things that I did went wrong, I lamented the difficulty of finding a hiding place.

From this time, I shook off the confusion and anxiety of this world, and cast aside that which entangled my heart.

6. 龍潭古舍 家嚴之丈席 東都新府 惟我之故鄕 率妻子還捿之日 己未之十月 乘其運道受之節 庚申之四月 是亦夢寐之事 難狀之言 察其易卦大定之數 審誦三代敬天之理 於是乎 惟知先儒之從命 自歎後學之忘却 修而煉之 莫非自然 覺來夫子之道 則一理之所定也 論其惟我之道 則大同而小異也 去其疑訝 則事理之常然 察其古今 則人事之所爲

The old house at Yongdam is the place where my father gained respect from many scholars for his great scholarly knowledge and virtue, and the ancient capital, Gyeongju, is my hometown. It was October, 1859 when I returned home with my wife and children. It was April 1860 when I learned my heavenly destiny and received the revelation of the Truth (the Way). It was an event like a dream, and it was an experience that was difficult to describe with words.

As I examined the great principles contained in the Book of Changes[77] and investigated the principles according to which the rulers of the Hsia, Yin, and Chou dynasties revered Heaven, I realized that former scholars followed the Will of Heaven. But I lament that later students forgot it.

As I examined the Way (revealed to me) by spiritual training, I discovered that it is not different from the law of Nature. When I examined Confucius' way, I realized that it has common points with our Way (Truth). As far as my own Way is concerned, it is largely similar to Confucius' way, but also somewhat different.[78] When I removed doubt, I realized that my Way is the most certain universal Truth. When I examined the history of past and present, I realized that my Way is ethical Truth for all humankind.

7. 不意布德之心 極念致誠之端 然而彌留 更逢辛酉 時維六月 序屬三夏 良朋滿座 先定其法 賢士問我 又勸布德

For a while, I put aside the idea of spreading the Truth and concentrated earnestly on spiritual training. As I postponed the propagation of Truth, the year of 1861 arrived. The month was June and the season was summer. As good friends came and filled the room, I established first the law of spiritual training. Wise scholars inquired about the Way and urged me to propagate it.

8. 胸藏不死之藥 弓乙其形 口誦長生之呪 三七其字 開門納客 其數其然 肆筵設法 其味其如 冠子進退 悦若有三千之班 童子 拜拱 倚然有六七之詠 年高於我 是亦子貢之禮 歌詠而舞 豈非仲尼之蹈

In my heart I had the elixir of life. Its shape was like spiral forms (弓乙, *gung eul*).[79] We chanted the incantation of immortality, which consists of twenty-one (Chinese) characters.

As I opened the door and received guests, their numbers were large, and I prepared the training hall with great joy. As the gentlemen came and went, the scene was like the great group of three thousand disciples of Confucius. The scene of the children bowing with proper gestures was like the recitation of poems by the children of a disciple of Confucius. Some of my followers were older than me. This was comparable to Tzu Kung, who was older than Confucius. The scene of our singing and dancing was like that of Confucius and his disciples.

9. 仁義禮智 先聖之所教 守心正氣 惟我之更定 一番致祭 永侍之重盟 萬惑罷去 守誠之故也 衣冠整齊 君子之行 路食手後 賤夫之事 道家不食 一四足之惡肉 陽身所害 又寒泉之急坐 有夫女之防塞 國大典之所禁 臥高聲之誦呪 我誠道之太慢 然而肆之 是爲之則

Humaneness, righteousness, propriety, and wisdom are the virtues taught by the former sages.[80] Keeping a good mind and having the right spiritual force are the virtues established only by me.[81] The initiation ceremony is a solemn vow to serve God forever. To remove all doubts is to keep sincerity.

To wear one's clothes and hat correctly is the conduct of the superior man. To eat on the road and to hold one's hands behind one's back are acts of the inferior man. In the home of believers, the harmful, bad meat of animals (i.e. dogs) is not to be eaten. And to sit suddenly in cold water is harmful. The evil act (sins against propriety) of married women is forbidden by the law of the nation. To recite the incantation with a loud voice while in bed is lazy behavior to our Way. Therefore, as I declare these teachings, make them the rules of life.

10. 美哉 吾道之行 投筆成字 人亦疑王羲之跡 開口唱韻 孰不服樵夫之前 懺咎斯人 慾不及石氏之貨 極誠其兒 更不羨師曠之聰 容貌之幻態 意仙風之吹臨 宿病之自效 忘盧醫之良名

How beautiful is our Way! Those who follow our Way are able to write as beautifully as Wang Hui-chi,[82] and they are able to sing beautiful songs, even though they may be low class laborers. Those who follow our Way and repent of their past mistakes do not desire the wealth of the rich man Sok-sung in ancient China, and those who have utmost sincerity for our Way do not envy the intellect of Sa-kwang of ancient China. The appearance of believers changes and becomes like the mystic sages, and as their long-term diseases disappear they will forget the names of famous doctors.

11. 雖然 道成德立 在誠在人 或聞流言而修之 或聞流呪而誦焉 豈不非哉 敢不憫然 憧憧我思 靡日不切 彬彬聖德 或恐有誤 是亦不面之致也 多數之故也 遠方照應而亦不堪相思之懷 近欲敍情而必不無指目之嫌 故作此章 布以示之 賢我諸君 愼聽吾言

However, in order to realize the Way and to establish Virtue, one must have the genuine sincerity and learn from the right person. Some people hear bad rumors and believe them, and some people hear the wrong kind of incantation and recite it. Isn't it a terribly wrong and sad thing?!

There is no day in which I do not think of my followers. I fear sometimes that our brilliant Way and Virtue may be falsified, since we are not able to be together now and believers are numerous. As we exchange news from a distance, it is difficult to suppress our longing to see each other. Although I want to have fellowship with you in a location nearby, there is danger of being watched by the authorities.[83] Therefore, I write and show this to you. All you gentlemen pay careful attention to my words.

12. 大抵此道 心信爲誠 以信爲誠 人而言之 言之其中 曰可曰否 取可退否 再思心定 定之後言 不信曰信 如斯修之 乃成其誠 誠與信兮 其則不遠 人言以成 先信後誠 吾今明諭 豈非信言 敬而誠之 無違訓辭

In our religion, the mind that believes has sincerity. If we analyze the term faith it is composed of man and word. Among words, some are true and some are false. Choose true words, and reject false words, and then think again and decide firmly. Faith is not believing any other words after a firm decision has been made. If one would practice in such a way, he will achieve sincerity. The principles of sincerity and faith are not so far apart. The word faith is based on the terms human and word, and the word sincerity is composed of word and achievement. Thus, first have faith and then sincerity. Now I have taught you clearly. Aren't they believable words? Have reverence and sincerity, and do not disobey my words of instruction.

# NOT SO, YET SO
(不然其然 *BURYEON GIYEON*)[84]

1. 歌曰 而千古之萬物兮 各有成各有形 所見以論之 則其然而似然 所自以度之 則其遠而甚遠 是亦杳然之事 難測之言 我思我 則父母在玆 後思後 則子孫存彼 來世而比之 則理無異於我思我 去世而尋之 則惑難分於人爲人

According to the words of a famous song, from the very beginning all things of the universe have had unique features and forms. If we are to describe them according to our observations, they are self evident manifestations. But if we are to determine their origins, they are very, very distant and, therefore, they are most difficult to determine and describe.

When I think of my present existence, I am aware that my parents preceded me, and when I think of my future, I am aware that my descendants will carry on through successive generations. When I think of my future, its principle does not differ from my thought about my present existence. However, when I consider past generations, questions arise in my mind, and I find it difficult to understand how the first parent of humankind became a human being.

2. 噫 如斯之忖度兮 由其然而看之 則其然如其然 探不然而思之 則不然于不然 何者 太古兮 天皇氏 豈爲人豈爲王 斯人之無根兮 胡不曰不然也 世間 孰能無父母之人 考其先 則其然其然 又其然之故也

Ah - such is my thought! When I consider obvious things, I find them easy to understand as self evident, but when I examine obtuse things, I find them difficult to understand, for they seem unknowable.

How is it so? How did Cheonhwangsi[85] become a man and king? Since he is known to have no origin, how could anyone not regard this as strange? In this world, no one could exist without parents. Therefore, when we consider the ancestors of each person, we can say that all exist because of self evident relations.

3. 然而爲世 作之君作之師 君者 以法造之 師者 以禮敎之 君無傳位之君 而法綱 何受 師無受訓之師 而禮義 安效 不知也不知也 生而知之而然耶 無爲化也而然也 以知而言之 心在於暗暗之中 以化而言之 理遠於茫茫之間

For the benefit of the world, kings and teachers have been produced. Kings should rule by law, and teachers instruct with propriety. Since the first king in the world had no previous king whom he succeeded, how did he receive the codes of law? Since the first teacher in the world had no predecessor who instructed him, from whom could he learn propriety and righteousness? This is indeed an unknowable thing. Did all these events happen because such leaders had knowledge from the moment of their birth, or because knowledge developed by itself? Even if one says that they had knowledge from the time of birth, at that stage our minds are still in darkness, and even if one says that all things happen by themselves, the Truth is far away and hard to reach.

4. 夫如是則不知不然故 不曰不然 乃知其然故 乃恃其然者也 於是 而惴其末究其本 則物爲物理爲理之大業 幾遠矣哉 況又斯世之人兮 胡無知胡無知數定之幾年兮 運自來而復之

Because people do not know why certain things came to be so, they cannot explain them. And because they also know why certain things are so, they affirm and maintain them.[86]

Therefore, if we study the fruits and root of all things, we can see how great and vast the material aspects and the principles of the universe are. How could people not know that the destiny of the world is determined, and the destiny arrives at its own time and repeats itself!

5. 古今之不變兮 豈謂運豈謂復 於萬物之不然兮 數之而明之 記之而鑑之 四時之有序兮 胡爲然胡爲然 山上之有水兮 其可然其可然 赤子之穉穉兮 不言知夫父母 胡無知胡無知 斯世之人兮 胡無知

聖人之以生兮 河一清千年 運自來而復歟 水自知而變歟 耕牛之聞言兮 如有心如有知 以力之足爲兮 何以苦何以死 烏子之反哺兮 彼亦知夫孝悌 玄鳥之知主兮 貧亦歸貧亦歸

The principles of the universe remain unchanged in the past and present. There are many things in the universe which are not so obvious. I shall consider, clarify, write, and reflect on them.

There is order in the four seasons. Why is it so? Really, why is it so? There is water on the top of mountains. How is it so? Really, how is it so? Very small children know their parents even though they cannot speak. Thus, why don't the people of this world know God: the source of their lives? There is a saying that every thousand years, when a sage is born, the Hwang-ha (Yellow River of China) becomes clean. Does destiny arrive and repeat itself, or does the water know and become clean by itself? The cows that listen to their masters' words and cultivate the farms seem to have minds and knowledge. These cows have the strength to work and live by themselves. Then, why do they suffer and die for men? There is a saying that crows bring food to their old mothers. Do they know filial piety and love? Swallows know their masters. No matter how poor their masters may be, they return to their home every year.[87]

6.  是故 難必者 不然 易斷者 其然 比之於究其遠 則不然不然 又不然之事 付之於造物者 則其然其然 又其然之理哉

Therefore, those things which are difficult to determine may be called "unknowable", and those things which are easy to determine may be called "self evident".[88] If we search for the distant source of all things, it appears again and again to be "unknowable." But if we consider the Creator as the source of all things, they appear be very much "self evident" and their origin becomes apparent.[89]

# POEMS, INCANTATIONS, AND OTHER WRITINGS

## ON BLESSING
(祝文 *CHUKMUN*)[90]

生居朝鮮 添處人倫 叩感天地盖載之恩 荷蒙日月照臨之德 未曉歸
眞之路 久沉苦海 心多忘失 今玆聖世 道覺先生 懺悔從前之過 願隨
一切之善 永侍不忘 道有心學 幾至修煉 今以吉朝良辰 淨潔道場 謹
以淸酌庶需 奉請尙饗

    I deeply appreciate that I was born in Korea and that I have experienced good relationships and received the blessings bestowed on me by Heaven and earth and the benefits of the sun and moon.
    However, I did not realize the way to the Truth but sank in this world of suffering, and my mind became impure.
    Now, in this latter day[91] I have met a Master who has realized the Truth,[92] I repent my past faults and want to do only good.
    From now on I will never forget how to serve God and I will do my utmost to study the Truth of the mind.
    Now, on a good day I clean the training room and offer pure wine and food, so please accept them.[93]

# INCANTATION
## (呪文 *JUMUN*)

呪文

先生呪文

降靈呪文
至氣今至四月來

本呪文
侍天主令我長生無窮無窮萬事知

弟子呪文
初學呪文
爲天主顧我情永世不忘萬事宜

降靈呪文
至氣今至願爲大降
本呪文
侍天主造化定永世不忘萬事知


**The Incantation of the Master:**

The incantation for the descent of the spirit:
The ultimate energy (of God) has reached me now; it is April.[94]

The main incantation:
By realizing that I have God within me,
I want to live eternally and know all truths.

## The Incantation of the Disciple:

The incantation of new member:
For God I will set my will and feeling, and forever
I will not forget God's grace, and I will do all things rightly.

Incantation for the descent of the spirit:
The ultimate energy (of God) is reaching me now;
I pray for its great descent.

The main incantation:
Realizing that I bear God within me,
I want to be transformed according to the will of God,
and I want not to forget God's grace forever
and want to know all truths.

# POEM ON THE ARRIVAL OF SPRING
(立春詩 *IBCHUNSI*)[95]

道氣長存邪不入 世間衆人不同歸

As my mind has been firmly set on the realization of the
Way for a long time, wrong thoughts cannot enter into my mind.

I will not tread the path that foolish people walk.

# ON DESTINY
(絶句 *JEOULGU*)⁹⁶

河淸鳳鳴孰能知 運自何方吾不知

平生受命千年運 聖德家承百世業

龍潭水流四海源 龜岳春回一世花

Who could know the time of the purification of Hwangho River and the singing of the phoenix?[97]

I do not know how destiny is shaped.

But the mandate of Heaven I have received is everlasting.[98]

The sacred and virtuous tradition of my family continues in my work.[99]

The waters from Yongdam[100] become the source of all the seas.

As the spring returns to Gumi Mountain,[101] flowers blossom throughout the whole world.

# THE POEM I RECEIVED FROM GOD
(降詩 *GANGSI*)[102]

圖來三七字 降盡世間魔

As I draw the twenty-one letters of the incantation,[103]
the evil forces of the world surrender.[104]

# PROVERBS
## (座箴 *JWAJAM*)[105]

吾道博而約 不用多言義

別無他道理 誠敬信三字

這裏做工夫 透後方可知

不怕塵念起 惟恐覺來知

My Way is comprehensive and great, yet also simple.

About truth, we do not use many words.

Also, my Way contains no special method of study or strange ideas.

It consists of the three (Chinese) characters:
sincerity, reverence, and faith.

Study diligently these principles and precepts.

Then, you can realize the Truth.

Do not be concerned with distracting thoughts,
but concentrate only on awakening your mind
and arriving at the knowledge of Truth.

# POEM IN RESPONSE TO GOD'S TEACHING
(和訣詩 *HWAGYEOL SI*)[106]

方方谷谷行行盡 水水山山箇箇知
松松栢栢靑靑立 枝枝葉葉萬萬節
老鶴生子布天下 飛來飛去慕仰極
運兮運兮得否 時云時云覺者
鳳兮鳳兮賢者 河兮河兮聖人
春宮桃李夭夭兮 智士勇兒樂樂哉
萬壑千峰高高兮 一登二登小小吟
明明其運各各明 同同學味念念同
萬年枝上花千朶 四海雲中月一鑑
登樓人如鶴背仙 泛舟馬若天上龍
人無孔子意如同 書非萬卷志能大
片片飛飛兮 紅花之紅耶
枝枝發發兮 綠樹之綠耶
霏霏紛紛兮 白雪之白耶
浩浩茫茫兮 淸江之淸耶
泛泛桂棹兮 波不興沙十里
路遊閑談兮 月山東風北時
泰山之峙峙兮 夫子登臨何時
淸風之徐徐兮 五柳先生覺非
淸江之浩浩兮 蘇子與客風流
池塘之深深兮 是濂溪之所樂
綠竹之綠綠兮 爲君子之非俗
靑松之靑靑兮 洗耳處士爲友
明月之明明兮 曰太白之所抱
耳得爲聲目色 盡是閑談古今
萬里白雪紛紛兮 千山歸鳥飛飛絶
東山欲登明明兮 西峰何事遮遮路

As I traveled to various places throughout the country,
I could see many streams and mountains.

Pine trees and big cone pine trees stand very green.

And there are so many branches and leaves.¹⁰⁷

The old crane gave birth to little ones
which are spread throughout the whole world.

They fly here and there and they adore the old crane greatly.¹⁰⁸

Fortune, fortune, did you receive it or not?

Time reveals the Truth to the person who is awake.

As the phoenix flew in, the sage was born.

As the Hwangho (Yellow) River is renewed, the sage is born.¹⁰⁹

As the peach and plum flowers blossom beautifully in the spring palace, the wise scholars and courageous youth are happy and joyful.

Through many valleys and toward lofty mountain tops, I climb step by step and make but a small sound.¹¹⁰

As the light of the new age is shining, it casts its light everywhere.

As all who learn the Truth experience the same sweet taste, their thoughts become as one.¹¹¹

Thousands of flowers blossom on a tree that is thousands of years old.

The moon that shines in the middle of the clouds of the world looks like a mirror.

The man who ascended to the pavilion is like the mystic who rides a crane.

The horse which is in the boat is like a dragon which ascends to Heaven.

Though the ordinary people did not study many books, their will can be as great as that of Confucius.

The flying things in the spring wind, they are really red flowers. The budding things on the trees, they are really green branches of the trees.

The falling and flying things in the winter, they are really white snow.

The wide and long things in nature, they are really blue rivers.[112]

Paddling a boat along a quiet river, I see no waves but a long sandy beach.

At a leisurely pace, I travel to various places.

The moon rises on the mountains, and the evening wind blows softly.[113]

As I behold the Great Mountain, I think of the time when Confucius went up to the mountain.[114]

As the clean wind blows quietly, I think of Master O Ryun's words about the realization of errors.[115]

The wide and large blue river reflects the pleasant party described in Soh Dong Pa's poem.[116]

The very deep lotus pond echoes the place Chou Lien Hsi (Ju Ryeom Gye) enjoyed.[117]

The green color of the bamboo trees reflects the purity of the superior man.

The green color of pine trees looks like a friend of that reclusive scholar who washed his ears.[118]

The brightness of the moon evokes the moon which Yi Tae Baek embraced.[119]

That which is gained by ear is sound, and that which is gained by eye is color.

All these converse about past and present.

As the white snow falls and scatters over thousands of miles, the birds that fly over a thousand mountain peaks stop flying.[120]

The bright sun is ascending in the eastern mountains.

How could the peaks of the western mountains stop the rise of the sun?[121]

# LAMENTING THE HASTY MIND OF THE DISCIPLES
(歎道儒心急 *TANDO YUSIMGEUB*)

山河大運 盡歸此道 其源極深 其理甚遠 固我心柱 乃知道味 一念在玆 萬事如意

The great destiny of the cosmos returns to this Way.[122] Its origin is extremely deep and far reaching and its principle is very great. When one's mind is firmly established, one can know the true taste of the Way. When one has a single minded devotion, all things will work according to the Divine will.[123]

消除濁氣 兒養淑氣 非徒心至 惟在正心 隱隱聰明 仙出自然 來頭百事 同歸一理 他人細過 勿論我心 我心小慧 以施於人

Cleanse impure energy[124] and nurture clean energy. One should have the utmost diligent mind but also an upright heart.[125] Then, the quiet wisdom will develop naturally. All the things that will happen in the coming age will return to one principle.[126] Do not discuss others' minor mistakes. Give others your wisdom even if it may be small.

如斯大道 勿誠小事 臨勳盡料 自然有助 風雲大手 隨其器局 玄機不露 勿爲心急 功成他日 好作仙緣

While we are working for such a great Way, we should not dwell on small and insignificant things. If we do our best when we face an important task, then certainly there will be help from God. Great ability depends on spiritual training. Even though the mysterious power of God may not manifest, do not have an anxious mind. On the day of accomplishment after spiritual training, there will be a great celebration in Paradise.

心兮本虛 應物無迹 心修來而知德 德惟明而是道 在德不在於人 在信不在於工 在近不在於遠 在誠不在於求 不然而其然 似遠而非遠

The mind is originally void and there is no trace of matter in it.[127] When the mind is cultivated one knows virtue, and when the virtue becomes bright it is identical with the Way.[128] The realization of the Way comes from the grace of God, not humankind. It is by faith, and not by study. The Way exists nearby, not in a distant place. The Way is realized by sincerity, not by a mere search. The Way was the same before all things existed and will remain constant after all things have ceased to exist. Therefore, the Way may appear to be distant but this is not really so.[129]

# WORDS ACCORDING TO DIVINE WILL
## (訣 *GYEOL*)[130]

問道今日何所知　意在新元癸亥年
成功幾時又作時　莫爲恨晚其爲然
時有其時恨奈何　新朝唱韻待好風
去歲西北靈友尋　後知吾家此日期
春來消息應有知　地上神仙聞爲近
此日此時靈友會　大道其中不知心

Today people ask about the Way and question: What is knowledge?

There is hope in the New Year.[131]

Success comes in due time, so there should be no regret when such a thing comes late.

Time has its own nature, thus, there is no use for regret.

In the morning of the New Year, we should sing and wait for the good wind.

Last year, friends visited us from the northwest.

Later I realized the significance of the meeting at our home.

As I can feel the arrival of spring, news of the arrival of the Paradise on Earth is near.

On this day, at this time, my soul friends are gathered together, and the great Way is present in our midst.

# COLLECTION OF WORDS
(偶吟 *UEUM*)[132]

南辰圓滿北河回　大道如天脫劫灰
鏡投萬里眸先覺　月上三更意忽開
何人得雨能人活　一世從風任去來
百疊塵埃吾欲滌　飄然騎鶴向仙臺
淸宵月明無他意　好笑好言古來風
人生世間有何得　問道今日授與受
有理其中姑未覺　志在賢門必我同
天生萬民道又生　各有氣象吾不知
通于肺腑無違志　大小事間疑不在
馬上寒食非故地　欲歸吾家友昔事
義與信兮又禮智　凡作吾君一會中
來人去人又何時　同坐閒談願上才
世來消息又不知　其然非然聞欲先
雲捲西山諸益會　善不處卞名不秀
何來此地好相見　談且書之意益深
不是心泛久不此　又作他鄉賢又看
鹿失秦庭吾何群　鳳鳴周室爾應知
不見天下聞九洲　空使男兒心上遊
聽流覺非洞庭湖　坐榻疑在岳陽樓
吾心極思杳然間　疑隨太陽流照影

The Southern Cross is rising, and the galaxy surrounds the north skies.

The great Way is free from calamity like Heaven itself.[133]

As I look in the distance with a mirror, the pupils of my eyes see in advance.

As the moon rises in the night, suddenly I have come to a realization.

Who can make a person alive with rain? I have lived my life as if chasing the wind.

By removing all the accumulated dust, I fly like a crane towards Paradise.[134]

There is no other reason for the bright moonlight in the clear sky. It is our custom to have a good laugh and good conversation on such occasions.

What does a man gain in this world when he is born?

On this day when questions are asked about the Way, we merely exchange our views.

I did not realize that the Truth resides in that point.

The will of my wise friends must be the same as mine.

Heaven produced all people and the Truth.

I do not know why everything has unique features and shapes.

If one does not violate the will of the heart, there will be no doubt in big or small issues.

Having wandered in strange places, I now yearn to return home and enjoy the old ways - especially on Cold Food Day[135].

Righteousness, faith, propriety and wisdom develop when you and I meet.

When was the time in which people were coming and going?

As we sit and talk leisurely, we wish a great sage would appear.

As I do not know the news of this world, I wish to hear what is happening.

My good friends gathered on the western mountain, where the clouds lifted.

Their names are not distinguished, because they do not make their good deeds known.

How did we come to this place and meet each other with such joy?

As we share good conversations and writings, their meanings are deeply profound.

I am not staying here very long because my mind is anxious and I want to meet wise friends in other places.

If the deer lost their garden in the Chin dynasty,[136] how can we make a large crowd?

The phoenix cried in the palace of Chou kingdom.[137] You should know its meaning.

I have not seen China, but when I have heard about it as "the Nine States,"[138] my mind has become excited.

I hear the sound of running water, but I realize that it is not Dongjeong lake.[139]

As I sit in front of the desk, I am wondering whether I am in Agyang Pavilion.[140]

My mind is thinking about the mysterious realm.

I am wondering whether it is like a shadow following the movement of the sun.

# THE FIRST EIGHT VERSES
## (前八節 *JEON PALJEOL*)[141]

1. 不知明之所在 遠不求而修我

If you do not know the location of the light of the universe,
do not seek it in a distant place, but find it within yourself by spiritual training.

2. 不知德之所在 料吾身之化生

If you do not know the virtue and grace of God,
think about the way our body and life came into being.

3. 不知命之所在 顧吾心之明明

If you do not know that God gave us life,
brighten your mind again and again.

4. 不知道之所在 度吾信之一如

If you do not know the Way,
examine whether your faith is steady and changeless.

5. 不知誠之所致 數吾心之不失

If you do not know whether your sincerity is real and ultimate,
examine whether you have lost the pure mind.

6. 不知敬之所爲 暫不弛於慕仰

If you do not know how much reverence you have for God,
do not be slow even for a moment in adoring him.

7. 不知畏之所爲 念至公之無私

If you do not know whether or not you fear God,
consider whether you are fair to others and not selfish.

8. 不知心之得失 察用處之公私

If you do not know whether your mind is fair or not,
then observe whether your mind is used for the good of others or for selfish purposes.

# THE SECOND EIGHT VERSES
(後八節 *HU PALJEOL*)[142]

1. 不知明之所在 送余心於其地

If you do not know the original light of the universe,
send your mind to that place.

2. 不知德之所在 欲言浩而難言

People do not know the virtue and grace of God,
because it is vast and difficult to discuss.

3. 不知命之所在 理杳然於授受

People do not know that God gave us life,
because how it is conveyed and how humans receive it is a mystery.

4. 不知道之所在 我爲我而非他

If you do not know the Way,
find it within yourself and nowhere else.

5. 不知誠之所致 是自知而自怠

If you do not know whether you have ultimate sincerity for God,
you should know that you may be lazy.

6. 不知敬之所爲 恐吾心之瘖昧

If you do not know how much you are honoring God,
you should fear that your mind may be dim and ignorant.

7. 不知畏之所爲 無罪地而如罪

If you do not know how much fear you have for God,
regard all places as sinful, though they may not be sinful.

8. 不知心之得失 在今思而昨非

If you do not know whether you have an unselfish heart or not, think now about your past mistakes.

## WRITING ON THEME
(題書 *JESEO*)[143]

得難求難 實是非難 心和氣和 以待春和

It may appear difficult to seek and gain, but actually it is not difficult.

Wait for harmony between your mind and God's mind and between your energy and Divine energy like the harmony of spring.[144]

# THE SONG THAT WE SING AT NIGHT
(詠宵 *YEONGSO*)[145]

也羞俗娥觀覆態　一生高明廣漢殿
此心惟有清風知　送白雲使藏玉面
蓮花倒水魚爲蝶　月色入海雲亦地
杜鵑花笑杜鵑啼　鳳凰臺役鳳凰遊
白鷺渡江乘影去　皓月欲逝鞭雲飛
魚變成龍潭有魚　風導林虎故從風
風來有迹去無迹　月前顧後每是前
煙遮去路踏無迹　雲加峰上尺不高
山在人多不曰仙　十爲皆丁未謂軍
月夜溪石去雲數　風庭花枝舞蝴尺
人入房中風出外　舟行岸頭山來水
花扉自開春風來　竹籬輝疎秋月去
影沈綠水衣無濕　鏡對佳人語不和
勿水脫乘美利龍　問門犯虎那無樹
半月山頭梳　傾蓮水面扇
烟鎖池塘柳　燈增海棹鉤
燈明水上無嫌隙　柱似枯形力有餘

Seeing the shameful actions of vulgar women, I spend my life as a bright light from the Gwanghan Palace in the moon.

Only the clean wind knows such a mind like mine and sends the white cloud to hide my face.[146]

As the lotus flower is reflected in the water, the fish in the pond looks like a butterfly that flies over the flower.

As the moonlight is reflected on the sea, the clouds also look like the earth.

A cuckoo sings on an azalea bush and a phoenix plays on a phoenix mound.

As a white crane crosses a river, it seems to ride on its own shadow.

As the moon moves across the sky, it seems to fan clouds to fly.

Fish play in the pond where they become dragons.

The wind seems to guide the tigers in the forest, and they seem to follow the wind.

When wind arrives, there is a sign, but when it departs there seems to be no sign.

When I look back in front of the moon, I find that I am still in front of it.

Smoke seems to block my path, yet there is no sign of smoke when I step on it.

Cloud is on the top of the mountain, but its height cannot be measured.

There are many people on the mountain, but they are not all called immortals or sages.

Ten people may look like strong men, but they are not all real soldiers.[147]

In the moonlit night the passing clouds seem to count the stones in the brook, and on the flower branches of the windy garden, the butterflies are dancing as if measuring the flowers.

When people enter a room, wind seems to exit.[148]

As a boat approaches the hillside, the mountain seems to come down to the water.[149]

The flower blossoms naturally, when the spring wind blows.

As the bamboo trees are shining, the fall moon passes.

My shadow is in the green water, yet my clothes are not wet.

I may meet a beautiful person in the mirror, but no conversation is possible.

Outside of the water it is difficult to find a beautiful dragon to ride.

It is best to hide oneself in a tree when a tiger attacks.[150]

The half moon above the mountain top is like a coarse comb. The leaning lotus flower on the water looks like a fan.

The willow tree next to the pond seems to sink because of the fog.

As the fog appears the fishing boats light up their lanterns.

As the lamp shines on the water, there is no room for fault and suspicion.

A pillar has the form of a decayed tree, but its strength still remains.[151]

# THE WAY OF WRITING
(筆法 *PILBEOB*)[152]

修而成於筆法 其理在於一心 象吾國之木局 數不失於三絶 生於斯 得於斯 故以爲先東方 愛人心之不同 無裏表於作制 安心正氣始劃 萬法在於一點 前期 柔於筆毫 磨墨 數斗可也 擇紙厚而成字 法有違於大小 先始威而主正 形如泰山層巖

The way of writing is attained by spiritual training. The reason for it is in one mind. The tree is a symbol of our country[153]. Three times our nation almost reached the end of its destiny, but all was not totally lost. Since I was born in the East and realized the Way in the East, I will work for the East first. People have different minds, but I shall love all of them and make transparent and fair rules of life.[154] With a peaceful mind and right energy one can draw a line, and all the Truths may be found in that one point. First one must make one's writing brush soft and grind the black ink tablet many times, and then one can write.[155] One must select thick paper to write on. There is a difference between great and small Truths. One should begin to write first with a solemn attitude and correctly, and then make the shapes like great mountains and lofty rocks.

# SONG ON HIGH AND FLOW
## (流高吟 *YUGO EUM*)[156]

高峰屹立 群山統率之像
流水不息 百川都會之意
明月虧滿 如節夫之分合
黑雲騰空 似軍伍之嚴威
地納糞土 五穀之有餘
人修道德 百用之不紆

The high mountaintop stands firmly, and it seems to lead many small mountains.

The flowing water does not rest, because water from many streams seems determined to gather at a certain appointed place.

The bright moon wanes at times and at times becomes full, and it is like strong men split at times and united at times.

The dark cloud hangs over the sky, and it is like the solemn march of an army.

Only by fertilizing the land, will there be a plentiful harvest for all kinds of grain.

Likewise human beings ought to cultivate the Way and Virtue in order to have no hindrance or problems in all their affairs.

## POEM WITH A SUDDEN REALIZATION
(偶吟 *UEUM*)[157]

風過雨過枝 風雨霜雪來
風雨霜雪過去後 一樹花發萬世春

The wind shook a tree and its branches, and rain also fell on them.

Then, storms and snow also rained down on them.

But after the storms and snow have passed, flowers will blossom on the tree, and then the whole world will be in spring.

# OTHER POEMS
(其他詩文 *GITA SIMUN*)[158]

纔得一條路　步步涉險難
山外更見山　水外又逢水
幸渡水外水　僅越山外山
且到野廣處　始覺有大道
苦待春消息　春光終不來
非無春光好　不來即非時
玆到當來節　不待自然來
春風吹去夜　萬木一時知
一日一花開　二日二花開
三百六十日　三百六十開
一身皆是花　一家都是春
瓶中有仙酒　可活百萬人
釀出千年前　藏之備用處
無然一開封　臭散味亦薄
今我爲道者　守口如此瓶

I found a narrow path and walked on the hazardous road step by step.

I saw one mountain after another and faced one river after another.

Fortunately, I crossed over one river after another, and I passed over one mountain after another.

At last, I arrived at a vast place and realized that there was a great Way.

I have anxiously awaited the news of spring, yet the spring light has not arrived.

It is not that I do not like the spring light.

It has not yet arrived, because it not yet the time.

When it is the right season for its arrival, it comes naturally without delay.

Last night the spring wind blew, and then all the trees in the world knew at once of the arrival of spring.

In one day one flower blossoms, and in two days two flowers blossom.

In 360 days 360 flowers blossom.

One person blooms like a flower, and the whole family is in spring.

In the bottle there is a mystical wine, and it could give life to millions of people.

It was brewed a thousand years ago, but I have stored it for a special and useful occasion.

If I open it once without a good reason, the smell will disperse and the taste will diminish.

Today the people who follow our Way should keep their mouth like this bottle.

# APPENDIX A

# CHONDOGYO: WHAT KIND OF RELIGION IS IT?

## HISTORY OF CHONDOGYO

### The founder, Suun Choe Je-u

Chondogyo (The Religion of the Heavenly Way) was founded by Choe Je-u in 1860. It is a unique religion, and was originally called Donghak (Eastern Learning).[159] Donghak was a movement against Christianity, which was called Seohak (Western Learning). The name was changed to Chondogyo in 1905 to signify that the movement was primarily religious in character.

While the traditional religions of Korea, such as Buddhism, Confucianism, and Taoism are of foreign origin, and shamanism is relatively common in many parts of the world, Chondogyo is a unique, modern religion that originated in Korea.

The founder, Choe Je-u (1824-1864), is usually called by his honorific name, Suun. He was born in Gyeongju, the famous ancient capital of the Silla kingdom. According to legend, he had a brilliant face and mind from birth. He lost his parents at an early age, and thus soon experienced the severe sufferings of life.

## Appendix A. Chondogyo: What Kind Of Religion Is It?

The social condition of Korea in the late Yi (Choseon) dynasty was also extremely difficult. There was political and social decay in the nation, and the traditional religions had lost vitality. Suun felt that there must be a new Way to save the nation and give hope to the masses. He felt that the social discrimination between the *yangban* (aristocrats) and commoners was especially unjust.

In search of a new Way, Suun wandered about the country, meditating in mountains and along river banks. He observed the political, social, and moral decay evident throughout the kingdom. After about twenty years of meditation, especially at Yongdam hut located in Mount Gumi in Gyeongju city, Suun received a revelation from God, who is called *Hanullim* in Chondogyo. Suun's special spiritual experience occurred on April 5, 1860, which is observed as the founding day of Chondogyo and the first year of the Chondogyo calendar. Suun claimed that he received the revelation about the *Cheondo (Chondo)*, the Heavenly Way, from God. The term *Cheondo (Chondo)* is the basis of the word Chondogyo. Suun was convinced that the Way or the Truth that he received from God was totally new, it had never been heard before nor was it comparable to any claims in other religions and philosophies.

After his revelatory experience, Suun continued with spiritual training for one year. After approximately one year, in 1861, he began to teach the Way he had realized. This teaching or preaching is called *Podeok*, which means spreading the truth and virtue. He taught that all men have divinity within them without distinction between the aristocrats and the commoners, implying that all men are basically equal. Such ideas had a great appeal to the masses in nineteenth century Korean society, who were yearning for the improvement of their lives and the new order of the world.

Because Suun's teaching attracted many followers, the ruling class of Confucian gentry and the government officials began to watch Suun and his new religious movement with suspicion. Therefore, in November of 1861, Suun left Gyeongju and hid himself in a small grotto called Uenjeogam in Namweon, Jeolla province. In this place Suun wrote important parts of Chondogyo Scripture, including *Nonhak-mun (Discussion of Learning)*, *Gweonhak-ga (Song of Encouraging Learning)*, and *Dosu-sa (Poem on Spiritual Training)*.

After one winter season, Suun returned to Yongdam, his hometown, but he encountered the persecution of government officials. Eventually Suun was arrested in December 1863 by the special government official sent by the royal court of the king and imprisoned in Daegu prison. He was executed on March 10, 1864 in Daegu for allegedly preaching heretical and dangerous teachings. Suun believed his death was in accordance with the Will of Heaven and considered his execution as ensuring his martyrdom.

Suun criticized the corrupt social condition of Choseon dynasty as well as the arrogant military system of the Western powers which were invading the East in his time. In response to these situations, Suun founded Donghak as a new system of thought and belief. Thus, Donghak was an indigenous Korean ideology, which attempted to give new hope to the masses and to protect the nation from foreign influence. However, Donghak was considered by the government authorities to be a dangerous movement, which might become a threat to the existing order of the dynasty. Eventually Donghak and its believers were severely persecuted by the government and many of them were martyred.

## Haeweol Choe Si-hyeong

Choe Si-hyeong (1827-1898) became the successor of Suun as the second leader of Donghak. He is usually called by his honorific name, Haeweol.

He was born in a poor and low class family, and his parents died while Haeweol was young. He worked as a laborer in a farm and also in a paper factory. In 1861 Haeweol went to Yongdam to meet Suun and soon he became a dedicated follower of Suun at the age of 35. He had an extraordinary zeal for the teaching of Suun and devoted himself diligently to spiritual training. He found in Donghak a religion that offered hope for those who suffered under the unjust, discriminatory class system of Yi-dynasty society. Like Suun, Haeweol possessed innate intellectual ability and memorized all of the teachings of Suun. He also had superb leadership ability.

After observing Haeweol's extraordinary zeal for Donghak and leadership ability for a while, Suun appointed Haeweol as his successor on August 14, 1863. Soon after Suun was arrested and executed by the government authorities, Haeweol was also pursued by the government authorities as the new leader of the movement. Thus, he hid himself in various places throughout different provinces, especially deep in the mountains such as Mount Taebaek and Mount Sobaek in Gangweondo, Gyeongsangdo, and Chungcheongdo. Haeweol hid himself for 36 years from the pursuit of the government authorities. During this period, he was not just hiding himself, but also propagating the teaching of Donghak throughout various provinces, expanding and strengthening the Donghak movement. During this period Haeweol collected the writings of his master, Suun, and published them as *Donggyeong Daejeon (The Great Scripture of Eastern Learning)* and *Yongdam Yusa (The Song of Yongdam)* in 1880 and 1881. Both of these books constitute the *Chondogyo Scripture*. This was probably his greatest and most enduring accomplishment.

Even in the midst of persecution by the government, Haeweol led the Donghak movement successfully for over thirty years and expanded the movement to the wider area of the country. However, the government persecution against the Donghak movement grew more intense.

Then, in 1894, there occurred a significant historical event called the Donghak Revolution. This revolt was organized by the members of the Donghak movement against the government in order to gain an apology for the government's wrong-doing against Suun, the founder, and to demand an end to its policy of persecution against the Donghak movement. The revolution started in Jeolla Province under the military leadership of Jeon Bong-Jun, but it was eventually led by the supreme command of Haeweol and quickly spread to many parts of the country. One reason for the initial success of the revolution was the support of the peasants, who were dissatisfied with the corrupt feudalistic system of Choseon dynasty under which they had been suffering for a long time. But soon the government called for the help of the Chinese and Japanese armies and, with their help, was able to subdue and defeat the army of the Donghak Revolution.

As the Donghak army was defeated, Jeon Bong-Jun was captured and executed, and the Gyoju (head of the religion), Haeweol, fled into hiding. Haeweol initially had not approved of violent revolution, but had reluctantly gone along with it when it was started by Jeon Bong-jun. Haeweol was also captured eventually by the military force of the government and martyred as the leader of the movement.

The significance of the Donghak Revolution is that the masses of peasants expressed, under the Donghak leadership, their deep dissatisfaction with the existing feudalistic system, and this soon occasioned the end of old Korea and the dawning of democratic movements within the Korean political and social system. Through the Donghak Revolution, the power of the ruling class began to fall and class boundaries were weakened. As a whole, the masses as well as the ruling class were awakened to the new reality of the rising spirit of democracy. The Donghak Revolution also occasioned not only the Sino-Japanese War but the eventual rule of Japan in Korea and the genesis of Korean nationalism.

## Uiam Son Byeong-hui

Son Byeong-hui (1861-1922) is called by his honorific name, Uiam, among the Chondogyo believers. It is said that he had a very strong character and passion for justice from childhood, and impressed everyone that he would become a great leader. He joined the Donghak movement at the age of twenty-two and quickly became the chief disciple of Haeweol by demonstrating his sincere faith, passionate zeal, and practical wisdom. He was also a very charismatic and able leader like his predecessors.

Uiam succeeded Haeweol as the third leader of Donghak at the age of 38 on December 24, 1898. Under his leadership, Donghak grew still larger. Uiam added to the works of his predecessors a more refined, modern, and stronger organizational structure, and demonstrated to the nation that Donghak/Chondogyo was a religious movement interested in the advancement of human dignity and freedom and a powerful organization working for national independence.

As the government persecution against Donghak grew, Uiam went to Japan, where he could learn more about the world affairs and the importance of the modern education of young people. Around the time of the Russo-Japanese War of 1904, he directed the key members of Donghak in Korea to establish the *Jinbohoe*, the Progressive Society. Through this organization, Uiam directed a nation-wide movement aimed at social improvement by reforming old customs. For example, thousands of Donghak/Chondogyo followers did away with the topknot and began wearing dyed rather than the traditional white clothes. This non-violent movement by the members of Donghak is called the *Gabjin* Social Reform Movement.

On December 1, 1905, Uiam changed the official name of the religion from Donghak to Chondogyo to identify it more strongly as a religious movement. This pronouncement of Uiam signified that Donghak/Chondogyo was changing from a passive, secret position to an active, visible position. When Uiam returned to Korea in January, 1906, he established the Chondogyo central headquarters in Seoul and church districts throughout the provinces. He organized the structure of Chondogyo with a modern system.

When Japan occupied Korea and began its brutal, inhumane colonial rule, Uiam prepared to organize a movement against Japanese colonialism and promoted the independence of Korea. He trained his followers through the 49 day spiritual training to have a strong mental readiness. On March 1, 1919, all the major religions of Korea as well as non-religious people of Korea participated in the nation-wide protest against Japanese rule. Uiam played the role of the main leader of this famous March First Independence Movement, which is observed as a memorial day by all people of Korea even today.

Immediately after the March First Movement, Uiam was imprisoned by the Japanese authorities, where he became ill. He was released because of illness, but he died at his home in 1922. The Declaration of Independence contains the spirit of Chondogyo concerning the fundamental dignity, freedom, and equality of all people. All the major religions of Korea acted in a common and united spirit to affirm the rights and freedom of the Korean people. Uiam's strong belief in man's essential dignity and the equality of all men motivated him to lead Chondogyo as a forerunner of the independence movement in Korea.

## Chunam Park In-ho and after

In 1908 Park In-ho became the fourth leader of Chondogyo, succeeding Uiam. His honorific name was Chunam. He was born on the first day of the second month in 1856 at the village of Makdongni, Jangchon Township, Deogsan District, Chungnam Province. At the age of twenty-nine the simple and amicable Chunam became a follower of Donghak in 1883. For the first ten years after joining he never once removed or changed his clothes and completely abstained from such things as fish, meat, alcohol, and tobacco while going about his daily regimen of strict and devoted training. One anecdote tells of how, fearful of falling into a deep sleep, he used a sickle for a pillow. After taking a brief nap with his head resting on this farm implement he awoke to resume his recitation of the Incantation of Twenty-One Letters. Under the guidance and direction of Haeweol he entered Gaseobsa Temple in Gongju for his 49 day training and other studies, and developed into an important Donghak leader. At the time of the Donghak Revolution he served as overall commander of Donghak forces in the Chungcheong Province area under the title Virtuous Supreme Superintendent (*Deogeuijeobju*, 德義接主). Later, in 1901, upon being named a Respected Leader of the Way (*Gyeongdoju*, 敬道主), he served in such capacities as Elder of the Church, advisor to Central Church Headquarters, Church chief financial officer, and as teacher of Chondogyo theology. On the tenth day of the twelfth month in 1907, he was appointed Vice Head of the Way, and little more than a month afterwards, on the eighteenth day of the first month in 1908, he was chosen to succeed in the line of Church leadership and so became the fourth head of Chondogyo under the new title Great Leader of the Way (*Daedoju*, 大道主).

Upon assuming his duties as Great Leader of the Way he reshuffled the leadership structure of Church Headquarters and spared no effort in working to increase church membership. However, in 1910, having been annexed by Japan, Korea suffered the pain and humiliation of occupation by Japanese imperial forces. In order to overcome such suffering Chunam, despite the oppressively prying eyes of the suspicious Japanese authorities, acted in accordance with Uiam's wishes in devoting his main efforts to publishing and education.

It was the construction of what was at the time a state of the art printing facility annexed to Church headquarters that provided Chondogyo with the necessary foundation to become a leading player in the Cultural Movement. Furthermore, he stood at the forefront in education for the Korean people by taking over and running Boseong School and Dongdeog Girl's School, as well as constructing and managing roughly 800 religious indoctrination centers and thereby contributing to society's national adult education campaign.

In order for Chondogyo to carry out its heavy responsibilities Venerable Teacher Chunam chose not to serve as a representative of the Korean people during the March First Independence Movement. Nevertheless he was one of a group of forty-eight people arrested by the Japanese police and taken to jail. When, in 1922, Uiam passed away, Chunam relegated the disposition of all future internal church matters to committee discussion, and for this he is remembered as a highly spiritual leader.

In 1938, with Japan's invasion and occupation of Manchuria and the growing severity of its militarist government, he called the regional church leaders together and ordered a special prayer for the destruction and ruin of imperial Japan. This was quite appropriately called the Muin (戊寅, sexagenary cycle year) prayer for the destruction of Japan (*Muinmyeolwaegido*, 戊寅滅倭祈禱).

Chunam never submitted to the harsh oppression of Japanese rule and continued to direct the Chondogyo Church until, on the third day of the fourth month in 1940, he passed away. He was 86.

After the Chunam's passing, leadership of the Church was determined through elections in accordance with the establishment of a church congress. The leader of Chondogyo, someone with spiritual qualities who is also a capable administrator, was elected to office every three years. Today members of this congress continue to manage and move Chondogyo forward by assembling every three years to elect a new church head and other leaders, and to attend to any other church matters.

## UNDERSTANDING CHONDOGYO SCRIPTURE

After 1860 Suun, Choe Je-u, wrote many pieces in order to teach his followers concerning important ideas and doctrines of Donghak/Chondogyo. He produced three kinds of writings. The first type consists of somewhat long pieces written in Chinese[160] to describe the essential ideas and truth of Donghak. They include *Podeok-mun (On Propagating Truth), Nonhak-mun (A Discussion on Learning), Sudeok-mun (On Cultivating Virtue),* and *Buryeon Giyeon (Not so, yet so).*

The second type of writing Suun composed was short verses in Chinese (*Hanmun*). These were written for spiritual training and practice. They include *Si-mun (Poetic Writing), Gyeol (Words according to Divine Will), Ju-mun (On Incantation), Paljeoul (Eight Verses), Pilbeob (The Way of Writing), Chuk-mun (On Blessing), Tando Yusimgeob (Lamenting the Hasty Mind of Disciples),* and *Jwajam (Proverbs).*

The third type of writing is composed in poetry/song style in the Korean language (*Han-geul*) for commoners to understand the ideas and meanings easily. They include *Yongdam-ga (Song of Yongdam), Gyohun-ga (Song of Instruction), Ansim-ga (Song of Comfort), Dosu-sa (Poem on Spiritual Training), Gweonhak-ga (Song of Encouraging Learning), Mongjung-noso-mundab-ga (Song of Dialogue between the Old and Young in Dream), Dodeok-ga (Song of Morality),* and *Heungbi-ga (Song of Parable).* In these songs and poems Suun conveys his central ideas and doctrines.

After the death of Suun, his writings in Chinese characters were collected by Haeweol and his disciples, and the collection was published as *Donggyeong Daejeon* (Great Scripture of Eastern Learning) in 1880 in the house of Kim Hyeon-su, who was a disciple in Inje, Gangweon-do province. Haeweol and his disciples collected the eight writings of Suun in Korean (*Han-geul*) and published the collection as *Yongdam Yusa* (The Songs that the Master of Yongdam Left).161 This was published in wood in Chungcheong-do province.

However, the original 1880 edition of *Donggyeong Daejeon* and the original 1881 edition of *Yongdam Yusa* do not exist today. The 1883 edition of *Donggyeong Daejeon* and the 1893 edition of *Yongdam Yusa* are the oldest extant editions.

The main parts of *Donggyeong Daejeon* consist of *Podeok-mun*, which contain Suun's teaching concerning spreading the truth of Donghak, *Nonhak-mun* and *Sudeok-mun*, which discuss the truth of Donghak, especially in comparison with and in contrast to Western Learning (Roman Catholicism) and Confucianism, and *Buryeon Giyeon*, which discuss the origin and nature of man and the world. *Donggyeong Daejeon* was written in Chinese mainly for the upper class intellectuals, who could read Chinese, while *Yongdam Yusa* was written in Korean mainly for the low class masses so that they can easily read and understand the message of Donghak.

Korean society in the 19$^{th}$ century when Suun lived was a class society even in the use of language. The upper, educated class used Chinese (*Hanmun*) to write and read, while the lower commoner class used Hangul, which is a pure Korean language in the colloquial style to speak, write and read. It was necessary for Suun to use both types of language to express his thought and communicate to the maximum number of Korean people.

The Korean educational system at that time was based on the Hanmun (Korean style of Chinese) system cultivated and enforced by the ruling intellectual class, which followed the Confucian philosophy and culture. The Confucian philosophical texts in Chinese were the main content of education for most students during the Yi/Joseon dynasty, since Confucianism was the state philosophy and religion of the dynasty. Suun learned Chinese from his father, Geunam-gong, who was known as a noted Confucian scholar. It was natural for Suun to use Hanmun to communicate his ideas to the intellectuals of his time. Suun sometimes used the Confucian terms to express his thought in *Donggyeong Daejeon*.

# APPENDIX B

# IMPORTANT TERMS AND IDEAS OF CHONDOGYO

## *Jigi* (至氣, The Ultimate Energy)

The term *jigi* appears at the beginning of the Chondogyo incantation, which reads: "The ultimate energy is arriving now; I pray for its descent." Suun interpreted the great descent of the ultimate energy as a harmonious union with it. The incantation of Donghak /Chondogyo is really a prayer for a spiritual identification with the energy and mind of Hanullim, which is a special term for God in Chondogyo.

Suun also explained the Ultimate Energy as follows:

*The Ultimate Energy is great and vast spiritual matter, and it touches everything, and nothing is outside its direction. It looks like having a form, yet it is form, and it seems to have a sound, yet it is without sound and it is invisible. It is really the original and ultimate energy.*

The above quotation from Suun means that the Ultimate Energy is the spiritual energy which permeates the whole universe, and it is related to and directs everything in the universe. The ultimate energy is the original and ultimate source of all beings and things. It is the ultimate being.

The Ultimate Energy is the energy of God, by which all things are made. God, Hanullim, exists and acts through the Ultimate Energy. God and the Ultimate Energy are inseparable. The Ultimate Energy is the mode of God's existence and acts. The energy of God is primarily a spiritual energy. However, since it penetrates into and is present in all things in the universe, it encompasses both the spiritual and material world. There is an organic relation between the ultimate spiritual energy and the material universe. All things in the universe are interrelated and form one great life system through the Ultimate Energy. The whole universe is a great organic life system. This is the Donghak /Chondogyo view of the universe.

According to Donghak/Chondogyo, all beings and things in the universe have the same root or source, which is the Ultimate Energy. Thus, human beings are not the only ones who should be respected. Instead, Chondogyo emphasizes the idea of respecting Heaven, respecting man, and respecting material things. This idea has a profound implication for respecting and protecting the environment. The modern world is facing a serious environmental problem because of the neglect and destruction of the environment by the careless behavior of a great number of people. The Chondogyo idea of respecting all beings and things offers a challenge to the modern world.

### *Si Cheonju* (侍天主, Bearing/Serving God Within Me)

*Si cheonju* means bearing and serving God, who is within one's own mind and heart. When Suun, Choe Je-u, had the ultimate spiritual experience on April 5, 1860, the first principle he received from God, Hanullim, was "my mind is your mind." He realized that the Absolute God, Hanullim, does not exist elsewhere externally, but dwells within his own mind and heart. Thus, he made the idea of *si cheonju (bearing and serving God within me)* a central idea of Donghak/Chondogyo. He stated in one of his writings as follows:

> *You, simple folks, what is your faith?*
> *Do not believe in yourselves, but believe only in God.*
> *He is within you; thus do not seek him in distance but in near place.*

The term, *si cheonju* appears in the *Incantation* and *Nonhak-mun* of *Chondogyo Scripture*. Here *Cheonju (Chonju)* literally means 'the Heavenly Lord.' The pure Korean term for it is *Hanullim*, which is used in *Yongdam Yusa (The Words Left at Yongdam)* by Suun and which is used today by Chondogyo believers when they address God.[162] It implies that the God of Donghak/Chondogyo is a personal God in distinction to the Neo-Confucian idea of Heaven as the cosmic principle or law.

Suun interpreted the term *si* as having the divine spirit internally and the realization of energy externally. In other words, bearing and serving God means the realization of inward spirituality and outwardly energetic life. It means that one has the mind of God within and the power of God. In this state man and God are one.

Suun stated that after one has the spirit of God within and the realization of energy of God, he can be firm and changeless in his belief and action. The believer who has realized the truth practices what he believes without change of mind. Bearing God also means restoring the mind of God in one's mind and heart. The state of bearing implies that one has a pure heart like that of a child. When one bears the mind of God, he realizes also that he becomes eternal like God is eternal.

Originally and potentially all men bear divine essence within their nature and mind. However, people lost their pure original nature because of the negative environment and their egotistic mind and life. Man can restore his original purity through spiritual training. Chondogyo calls this realization "bearing God." This state is the state of realization of the authentic self, which is one with God in essence. The moment that one bears God within, he realizes he is eternal as God is. This is the concept of man in Donghak/Chondogyo.

Also in this idea of *si cheonju*, one can find that the God of Donghak/Chondogyo is primarily an immanent being, which exists within human heart and mind. The transcendent God, who is the object of worship and from whom all things originate and from whom Suun received the revelation, is not denied. But the immanent God, who is within human heart and mind, and who is sometimes identified with the universe, is emphasized in Donghak/Chondogyo.

## *Susim Jeonggi* (守心正氣, Keeping the Pure Mind and Having Right Conduct)

Suun, Choe Je-u, traveled throughout the country and observed the corrupt and chaotic situation of Korean society of the late Yi/Joseon dynasty which was based on Confucianism. The social and political decay caused by the corrupt ruling class as well as the egotistic behaviors of people in general dismayed Suun. He also observed critically the influence of the West, including the influence of Roman Catholicism in Asia and especially in Korea.

Suun thought that the main reason for the social problems of Korea was the egotistic mind and conduct of people from the high to low level of society. He said: "Each person has only a selfish mind." He saw the problem of society from a moral and religious point of view. He believed that the solution for the social problems of the nation is discarding the selfish mind by believing and having reverent fear of God.

Suun used a special term, *susim jeonggi*, as a solution for correcting the moral problem of society. It means to keep the original pure mind which one received from God and to have right conduct. He urged his followers to practice humaneness, justice, propriety, and wisdom, which are the four virtues of the superior man taught by Confucius, who is respected as a sage in Korean society as much as in China. Suun believed that the four virtues of humaneness, righteousness, propriety, and wisdom are universal virtues for mankind, including Korean society.

Suun taught that in order to practice the Confucian virtues of humaneness, righteousness, propriety, and wisdom, people need to cultivate and practice *susim jeonggi*. He said: "Humaneness, righteousness, propriety, and wisdom are taught by the sage (Confucius), but *susim jeonggi* is invented only by me." This statement may mean that the Confucian virtues are important, but the practice of the Confucian virtues depends on the spiritual cultivation of the pure mind and the cultivation of an upright moral character.

Based on Confucius' idea of the four virtues, Mencius taught that all men have the four original feelings; the feeling of commiseration, the feeling of shame and dislike (based on the ideal of righteousness), the feeling of respect (propriety), and the feeling of right and wrong, which constitutes wisdom. According to him, these feelings are innate, that is, all men are born with them, and they are endowed by Heaven.

Suun's idea of *susim jeonggi* is similar to Mencius' idea of the four original feelings. However, Suun's idea is more spiritual than Mencius' idea, for Mencius' idea is primarily ethical in nature. According to Suun and Donghak/Chondogyo, the key point of *susim* is to realize that man has an original pure divine nature, but since it is lost because of his own selfishness and negative influence from outside, he needs to restore it and preserve it through spiritual training. *Jeonggi* means having right spiritual energy, which translates into morally right action. It also means constant spiritual and moral exercise. For Donghak/Chondogyo *susim jeonggi* is a spiritual and moral discipline, by which one realizes that God is within us and restores the divine mind and lives a morally upright life.

In order to achieve *susim jeonggi*, one must have the attitude and mind of reverent fear of God, according to Suun. Then, one can truly practice the discipline of the pure mind and live a morally upright life. The ultimate result of the practice of *susim jeonggi* is the achievement of *si cheonju*, oneness with Hanullim. Many so-called wise men of Suun's time in Korea were hypocritical, having no real fear of God. Thus, he criticized as follows:

> *The so-called successful wise men of our Eastern country call themselves as morally superior man. These unenlightened people may know a thousand things, yet they do not have the reverent fear (of God). Thus, what value does such knowledge have?*

In the above statement, Suun was criticizing the Confucian scholars of his time, who called themselves the superior men (*chun tzu*), but their actions were hypocritical. They could explain the important ideas of Confucianism, but their actions were superficial and their conduct was merely formalistic. Many Confucian scholars of nineteenth century Korea were following the Neo-Confucianism of Chu His (Zhu Xi), and their metaphysical theories were abstract and had no dynamic power in the lives of the common people. Suun claimed that no matter how much the Confucian scholars knew, their ideas had no curing power for the ills of society. In Suun's view these scholars knew much about their own metaphysical theories, but they were ignorant and unenlightened people, for their knowledge had no value to cure the social problems.

Suun proposed the idea of 'reverent fear' (of God) as the solution for overcoming the Confucian formalism. When people have the reverent fear of God, they can restore and preserve their original pure mind, and they can perform morally upright acts. This discipline of *susim jeonggi* is considered the solution of Donghak/Chondogyo for the problems of Korean society.

Suun also mentioned that people were not following the Principle of Heaven and not obeying the Will of Heaven, because they were basically selfish in their search for success and happiness. Hence, for the whole world *susim jeonggi* is the solution, by which each person can restore the original pure mind, and the nation can overcome social and moral problems, and mankind can restore the authentic morality. According to Donghak/Chondogyo, Suun's idea of *susim jeonggi* is the way to overcome all the crisis and problems of mankind and bring peace to the world, for it is the way of recreating the pure mind and good morality of mankind.

## *Muwi Ihwa* (無爲而化, Natural Becoming)

Suun continued with spiritual training for approximately one year after his enlightening religious experience of 1860. After that period of spiritual training, Suun pronounced that the Way he realized is identical with the principle of nature. He told his disciples that his Way is *muwi ihwa* (natural becoming).[163]

*Muwi ihwa* as the principle of nature is also the way of God, according to Donghak/Chondogyo. While Lao Tzu, the founder of Daoism, believed that *wu-wei (muwi* in Korean) is the way of nature, the way of Dao, Suun asserted that it is also the way of God, Hanullim. While Daoism emphasizes union with Dao/nature, Chondogyo emphasizes oneness with God as the ultimate state of being.

Suun stated in *Nonhak-mun*: "My Way is *muwi- ihwa.* If one keeps the pure mind and practices right action, he will have a good nature.... and will be transformed naturally." According to Suun, it is necessary to actively cultivate the pure mind and the right conduct in order to achieve the natural and authentic state of being and living. Human beings initiate the spiritual training of cultivating the pure mind and actively cultivate moral conduct, and then God's gracious help arrives. Through human effort and the divine grace, *muwi-ihwa* is achieved.

Thus, the Chondogyo idea of *muwi ihwa* is somewhat different from the Taoist idea of *wu-wei,* although there is some similarity between them. The similarity is that both Daoism and Chondogyo emphasize the natural becoming or natural transformation and natural life. The difference, however, is that Daoism does not emphasize human effort, while Chondogyo emphasizes it as a means to attain the goal of becoming natural.

*Muwi ihwa* is the authentic way of life according to Donghak/ Chondogyo. Through it one can reach the state of God and the kingdom of Heaven. Human life in the highest level is natural and effortless. However, to arrive at this level, one must practice the spiritual training of cultivating the pure mind and right conduct. After human effort and divine grace, the level of natural and spontaneous life is achieved. In Donghak/Chondogyo this natural life is the authentic way of life, since in this state all the enlightened people can live morally pure lives without unnatural effort.

## *Buryeon Giyeon* (不然其然 Not So, Yet So)[164]

*Buryeon Giyeon* is a philosophical idea of Donghak/Chondogyo. It makes certain difficult and paradoxical ideas such as *si cheonju* (Bearing God; man has divinity within) conceivable and understandable. In one of his writings,[165] Suun mentioned that the eternal and infinite truth he discovered consists of the characteristic of *buryeon giyeon*, that is, not apparently obvious, yet clearly and apparently real. He continued to state that when he searched the truth with the dialectical method of *buryeon giyeon*, he realized that he is eternal in the eternal universe. Suun emphasized that the truth of Donghak/Chondogyo needs to be understood through the dialectical method. In other words, the eternal truth may appear to be obvious and clear sometimes, but sometimes it is not so clear and obvious. Both negative and positive aspects, both non-apparent and apparent aspects of the truth must be observed and dealt with.

According to Suun, the finite human being can realize that he can become eternal and infinite in the infinite universe when he uses the dialectical vision of *buryeon giyeon*. Also the finite human life can be transformed into eternal life, when one used the dialectic of *buryeon giyeon*, according to Donghak/Chondogyo. This is a mystical idea, for it involves some kind of intuitive union between the human and divine, and between the finite and the infinite. Suun's statement of "eternal self in the infinite and eternal universe" is the ultimate mystical expression, which is possible only through the dialectic of *buryeon giyeon*.

Suun also elaborated *buryeon giyeon* in *Donggyeong Daejeon* as follows:

Mind originally has no shape or form and is invisible, and it appears empty, and it has no trace, when it deals with all things. However, only when the mind is cultivated, one can know the Truth and grace of God. When the grace of God is brightly known, it is the Way or Truth. The fact that we know and realize the Truth depends on the divine grace, and it is never by other human being. The realization of Truth is possible when one accepts the teaching of God, and it does not come from mere study. Furthermore, the Way is near, and it is not in a distant place. It can be reached by the sincere and earnest heart and mind, and not by mere search. The Truth is the same whether it was before all things were made (*buryeon*) or after all things were made (*giyeon*). Therefore, the Way (Truth), which is the ultimate principle by which all things exist and all things are understood, is not in a distant place, but in our minds and lives.

Some of Suun's disciples were complaining and lamenting that the new world order according the Way of their master was not arriving quickly. Suun wrote for them *Tando Yusimgeob (Lamenting the Hasty Mind of Disciples)*, in which he instructed that it is important to cultivate a right mind and heart, and to realize that the Way (truth) is not in a distance place but in one's own mind. Suun taught them that the truth of Donghak seems to be not obvious or apparent, but it is obvious and apparent. He told them *buryeon giyeon* (not so obvious, yet obvious) is an important way of understanding the truth of Donghak.

Suun wrote an essay on *Buryeon Giyeon* in order to explain this point at length. In it Suun said that when we look at all things in the universe, the external phenomena are obvious and apparent, but if we search for the ultimate origin of all things, asking how they came into existence and from whence they came, the answer is not obvious nor easy. Similarly, when we ask about the origin of our existence, we know obviously and clearly by experience that we came from our parents, but if we go back to the ultimate origin of human beings, asking from whence the first human being came, the answer is not obvious, and it is difficult to know, according to Suun.

Therefore, according to Suun, that which can be understood and explained easily by the ordinary human experience and reason is *giyeon*. And that which cannot be understood and explained by the ordinary human experience and reason is *buryeon*. According to Suun, we usually live in the phenomenal world of ordinary experience, which is *giyeon*. However, ultimately and in the deepest level of our being we live in the world of *buryeon*, which lies beyond the realm of the ordinary sense experience.

However, through the transformation of understanding, *buryeon* can become *giyeon*. According to Donghak, we know the father of our father is our grandfather, but if we trace this line of thought to the first grandfather of human beings, it becomes *buryeon*, that which is not obvious but difficult to know. However, if we transform our mind and rely on the idea of the providence of God as the Creator, and think that the first grandparents of human beings received life from God, Hanullim, the origin of all things can be changed from *buryeon* (not so obvious) to *giyeon* (obvious). According to Donghak/Chondogyo, such a transformation of our consciousness is necessary. Such a transformation of consciousness is the way of restoring the original nature of man which is damaged by bad habits and bad environment.

The ultimate task of each believer in Donghak/Chondogyo is to restore the original nature of man endowed by God called Hanullim and to realize that God dwells in each person's heart. That is the central meaning of *si cheonju* (I bear and serve God within me). For Suun and his followers, the idea of *buryeon giyeon* was an important way of knowing and realizing *si cheonju*.

According to Donghak/Chondogyo, the ideal new world order can come only through *si cheonju*. It means that when all men restore the God-given original pure nature, becoming God-possessed people and live morally pure lives in accordance with the original pure nature, the kingdom of Heaven will be realized. The idea that the infinite God dwells in the finite human being implies that there is a mystical oneness between man and Hanullim. From this idea the idea of eternal life is also conceived. When Suun received the revelation from Hanullim, he was told by him: "You too will have eternal life and you will spread the truth to the whole world."

On the basis of Suun's idea of *si cheonju* (侍天主, I bear/serve God within me), Haeweol, the successor and disciple of Suun, developed the idea of *in jeuk cheon* (人卽天), which literally means that man is Heaven. Uiam, Sohn Byeong-Hui, the successor of Haeweol, developed the term *in nae cheon* (人乃天) which also means that man is Heaven (God). Uiam's term *in nae cheon* has become a central creed in Chondogyo. Thus, these terms and ideas signify a mystical union of man and Hanullim.

According to Donghak/Chondogyo, man needs to go beyond *giyeon* in order to realize the oneness of man with Hanullim and to realize the eternal life through bearing divinity. If one's thinking remains on the level of *giyeon* concerning his existence, it is only life and death, and life is no more than a brief physical existence. However, if he thinks about his existence from the perspective of *buryeon*, he can realize that human life has an eternal quality. Suun said: "I am eternal in this eternal universe." To realize the eternity of human life, one needs to have a dialectical vision of *buryeon giyeon*, according to Donghak/Chondogyo.

Thus, Suun emphasized that the way for realizing *si cheonju* (I bear/serve God within me) is through the dialectical consciousness of *buryeon giyeon*. Through the purification of mind and cultivating the right conduct, people can realize *si cheonju*. When people have realized the state of *si cheonju*, they have restored their original pure mind and they would live a morally pure life, and then the kingdom of Heaven will arrive on earth. To achieve this goal of life, the *buryeon giyeon* way of thinking about the important truths is necessary, according to Donghak/Chondogyo.

Therefore, *buryeon giyeon* has become the most important epistemological method of understanding truth in Donghak/Chondogyo. The important ideas of Donghak/Chondogyo, such as *si cheonju*, God (*Hanullim*), man's oneness with God (*in nae cheon*, which literally means that man is God), and man's relation to the universe, can be understood only through the dialectical epistemology of *buryeon giyeon* and the spiritual enlightenment, according to Donghak /Chondogyo.

## *Donggwi Ilche* (同歸一體, Returning to the Origin and Becoming One)

*Donggwi Ilche* literally means "Returning to the origin and becoming one." It actually means the ultimate unity of all people. This is an eschatological vision of Suun concerning the future of mankind. According to Suun, the present world is corrupt and decayed, because people disregard the Principle of Heaven and disobey the Will of Heaven, living according to their selfish interests. Suun was aiming at establishing the new world order by recreating human minds and hearts.

Suun used the phrase, *hucheon gaebyeok* (後天開闢) for the recreation of the future world. It means not only the recreation of the material, physical world, but also the recreation of human spirit. Suun emphasized especially the recreation of human minds and hearts, by eliminating the corrupt minds of people because of selfishness. According to Suun, when the human mind is purified through spiritual training, it is transformed into the mind of Hanullim (God). This is the recreation of human spirit. The recreated person is one who has God within himself (*si cheonju*), and at this point, human will becomes one with the will of God. Such a person is also called *jisang sinseon* (地上神仙), which means literally "a divine person on earth." Actually this means that such a person's life is like living in paradise on earth.

Suun said in one of his writings that any one who becomes a member of Donghak becomes the superior man and becomes a divine person in paradise on earth. Suun is using here the Confucian term, the superior man (*gun-ja* in Korean; *chun-tzu* in Chinese) and the Taoist term *sinseon*. Suun advocated that any human being can become the superior man regardless of social ranking and class membership, and unlike the reclusive Taoist sages who lived solitary lives in the mountains, Donghak believers live the sage's life in the real world of people.

The real superior men and sages are the members of the ideal community, which is the paradise on earth. The ideal human community

## Appendix B. Important Terms and Ideas of Chondogyo 75

is the world of recreated human beings, which is the world of *donggwi ilche*, the united community of mankind. The members of this community reject all individualistic selfish interests and surrender their will to the good of the whole community, which is identical with the will of God. This ideal community of *donggwi ilche* is the paradise on earth, where the members lose interest in their individuality and see all things for the interest of the whole community. When people have the mind of *donggwi ilche*, the interest of 'I' and 'me' is transformed into the interest of 'we' and 'us.'

When people cultivate and restore the pure original nature of man and cultivate the good moral conduct, they realize the state of *si cheonju* (bearing God in one's mind and heart), according to Donghak/Chondogyo. Such people are the members of this community of paradise on earth, which is the community of *donggwi ilche*, where people are united for the common good, happiness, and peace. This is the ultimate vision of the kingdom of heaven on earth for Donghak/Chondogyo.

# ENDNOTES

1) *Podeok-mun* (布德文) literally means "Writing on spreading virtue," but its meaning here is spreading the Chondogyo truth, that is, propagation or evangelism. It was written in the spring of 1861.

2) In the original text God is called *Cheonju* (天主) which is *Hanmun* (Korean version of Chinese), in which *Podeok-mun* was written. However, today Chondogyo uses the Korean (*Han-geul*) word *Hanullim* for God.

3) The term *johwa* (造化) is used in the text to express the development of all things in the universe. It can be translated as "making and changing" or "creation and evolution" of all things in nature by God's power. The idea includes both creation and evolution.

4) The Heavenly Way or the Way of Heaven in Korean is *Cheondo* (天道, *T'ien-tao* in Chinese). It is one of the most important ideas in Chondogyo. It means the law of the universe, by which all things originate, move, and change. The name Chondogyo is based on it.

5) The Will of Heaven in Korean is *Cheonmyeong* (天命, *T'ien-ming* in Chinese). In Chondogyo it means the Will of God, which controls the human mind and human affairs as well as the movement of the universe. It is basically the same idea as the Way of Heaven.

6) The Principle of Heaven in Korean is *Cheonri* (天理, *T'ien-li* in Chinese). It can be regarded as a synonym for the Way of Heaven and the Will of Heaven.

7) The superior man is a translation of *gunja* (君子, *chun-tzu* in Chinese), which is a central idea in Confucianism. The superior man in Confucianism is superior in character and conduct, embodying the virtues of humaneness, righteousness, propriety, and wisdom.

8) The Heavenly Virtue or Virtue of Heaven is the translation of *Cheondeok* (天德). It implies that Heaven or God has moral virtue, which is the source, model, and basis of the moral virtues of man.

9) The Westerners here refer to the Christian missionaries, the Western merchants who came to China, and the Western military forces which defeated China in the Opium War in the middle of the 19th century. The world in the text means China. Suun heard the news about these events in China and was deeply concerned about the future of Korea.

10) Here, Suun is describing his mystical experience of receiving God's revelation.

11) *Sangje* (上帝, *shang-ti* in Chinese) is a name of God as the Supreme Being in Chinese and Korean traditions.

12) Talisman is the translation of *yeongbu* (靈符), which may also be translated as 'spiritual symbol'. Mystical medicine here is a translation of *seonyak* (仙藥), which has a Taoist flavor.

13) The Great Ultimate is a translation of *taegeuk* (太極, *t'ai-chi* in Chinese). It means the ultimate source of the universe or the ultimate reality.

14) *Gung gung* (弓弓) is the symbolic term for eternity. The pictorial forms of the Great Ultimate and *gung gung* symbolize the infinite and ultimate source of the universe or the Ultimate Reality or the mind of God. *Gung* is the shape of archery.

15) Illness here means both physical and spiritual illness of the people as well as the social illness.

16) Incantation here means a chant, which is a very important part of Chondogyo ceremonies. The Chondogyo incantation is a formula of mystical words, which is repeatedly chanted to produce a mystical experience or to honor God.

17) Suun wrote the talisman (mystical symbol) on a paper and probably burned it and swallowed it with water.

18) Evil things may mean epidemic disease or moral corruption in society; the latter may be the real meaning.

19) 'The world' in the original text actually means 'China.'

20) "Supporting the nation and comforting the people" (*boguk anmin*, 輔國安民) is an important idea in Donghak/Chondogyo. It was one of the main ideas on which Donghak/Chondogyo was founded.

21) The change of destiny for individuals and dynasties was an important concept in Korea as well as in China, which is related to the Will of Heaven (天命, *T'ien-ming* in Chinese). According to Suun in this text, the old age (world) is about to end and the new age is dawning, and yet the ignorant people are unaware of the signs of the changing times. The implication here is that Suun is bringing the truth of the new age.

22) 'Truth and virtue' here may be rendered simply as morality or moral truth.

23) Written in February 1861.

24) 'The Heavenly Way' or the way of God is formless and invisible, but it has traces in all things in the universe.

25) 'The nine stars' generally refers to the entire sky.

26) 'The nine provinces of ancient China, which also implies the entire earth.

27) 'The eight trigrams (eight symbols) represent the eight essential principles of the universe in I Ching (the Book of Changes).

28) Numbers and principles in I Ching are keys, according to which the waxing and waning and all movements and changes in the universe are interpreted.

29) *Yin-yang* is an important idea in Korean tradition as well as in the Chinese tradition. *Yin* is the negative principle and *yang* is the positive principle.

30) The five agents are water, fire, wood, metal, and soil, which are the five essential components of the universe.

31) The reason that many people do not understand the cause of the phenomena of nature may be because they lack faith and correct knowledge of God.

32) April 1860 is the time when Choe Suun received the revelation and founded Donghak/Chondogyo. Around or before this time, China was defeated by the British military forces in the Opium War, and Suun and many Koreans were concerned and worried that the Western powers may conquer Korea any time.

33) 'Western Way' and 'holy religion' are synonymous with Roman Catholicism.

34) Here Suun is describing his mystical experience.

35) This is a mystical statement. The original and pure mind of man is identical with the mind of God, according to Chondogyo.

36) In the original text, The Spirit is *gwisin* (鬼神), which literally means ghost or spirit. But in this context, it can be translated as the Spirit or God, for Chondogyo affirms monotheism, rejecting the superstition of believing in ghosts or spirits.

37) The Principle of Nature is the same as the Way of Nature or Natural Way, which is an important idea in Chondogyo.

38) *Jigigeumji weonwi daegang* (至氣今至願爲大降), which means "I pray for the great descent of the Ultimate Energy now," is the technique of receiving the Spirit, which is actually the first part of the Incantation; *Sicheonju johwa jeong* (侍天主造化定), which means "God is within us and all are made well," is the second part of the Incantation; and *yeongse bulmang mansaji* (永世不忘萬事知), which means "eternally not forgetting and being aware of all things," is the poem of "Not Forgetting (God)," which is the last part of the Incantation. The entire Incantation consists of twenty-one Chinese characters.

39) The twenty-one character (Chinese) incantation is repeated by Chondogyo believers many times each day, especially during worship services, and it is probably the most important spiritual practice in Chondogyo.

40) Here Suun might have thought that the ultimate truth of both Christianity and Chondogyo are identical, although their doctrinal teachings are different.

41) The term natural way in the original text is *muwi ihwa* (無爲而化), which literally means "change without action." This is an important idea in Chondogyo. It means the way of God and the universe. It is a spontaneous way. Muwi (wu-wei in Chinese) is an important idea in Taoism. Here one may find a Taoist influence on Chondogyo thought.

42) The Heavenly Way (*Cheondo*) here means the Ultimate Reality and the ultimate source of all things. Both Eastern and Western learning are methods of reaching *Cheondo*.

43) There were incantations in the ancient past as well as today, as people prayed to gods for blessings.

44) *Ji* (至) means ultimate or extreme.

45) *Gi* (氣) means the vital force or energy. *ji-gi* (至氣), then, means the Ultimate energy, which is the energy or vital force of God. *Ji-gi* in the original text is described as *heo-ryeong* (虛靈), which means "spirit like void", that is, invisible, vast, and mysterious.

46) In this verse, some important terms in the incantation are explained. *Si* (侍) here can be translated as 'bearing or serving someone with respect'.

47) *Ju* (主) literally means lord or master.

48) *Johwa* (造化) means making, becoming, or transformation of all things.

49) *Jeong* (定) literally means to decide or settle.

50) *Yeongse* (永世) literally means eternal age or long time.

51) *Bulmang* (不忘) literally means not forgetting.

52) *Mansa* (萬事) can be translated as all things.

53) *Ji* (知) means knowledge or wisdom.

54) The oneness of the mind of God and the mind of man is an important idea in Chondogyo as well as in Confucianism.

55) Here the Confucian term, *chun-tzu (kun-ja* in Korean) is used.

56) Here the vital force or energy (*gi* in Korean; *ch'i* Chinese) is one of the most important ideas in Chondogyo. It sometimes means the energy of God.

57) "Success (good) and failure (evil)" is a liberal translation of *seong-swoe* (盛衰), which literally means waxing and waning.

58) Suun is stating here that his Way is an entirely new Truth and, therefore, some people doubt, disbelieve, and disparage it.

59) Here Suun is stating that only those who sincerely believe and practice his Way can have good and effective result, while those who merely listen without sincere heart and without practice can only experience futility and emptiness.

60) This statement means that God's spirit is given or descends upon anyone who sincerely seeks regardless of their moral background and status.

61) Here the disciples are asking whether good fortune and misfortune are not dependent on one's good and evil conduct. According to the Chondogyo idea of the revolutionary new age, individualistic good fortune and misfortune are no longer important, for all eventually return to the origin and become one (*donggwi ilche,* 同歸一體).

62) Yao and Shun were the virtuous rulers, according to the ancient Chinese legend.

63) Written in June 1862.

64) This sentence in the original text is written as *weon-hyeong-i-jeong* (元亨利貞) *cheondo ji sang* (天道之常). *Weon* (元) means beginning or origin and it is represented by spring, when all things are born or renewed. *Hyeong* (亨) means flourishing without hindrance and it is represented by summer, when all things grow and flourish. *I* (利) means profit or gain and it is represented by autumn, when all things bear fruits. *Jeong* (貞) means firmness or steadfastness and it is represented by winter, when all things are harvested and stored and firmly established. These four ways of nature are also the four virtues of life, and they are the unchanging, constant way of Heaven (Cheondo), the way of the universe.

65) Ancient King here refer to kings like king Mun (文王) of the Chou dynasty in China.

66) Suun's ancestor, General Ch'oe Chin-ip, made important contributions to the nation in the wars against foreign invasions, and was killed in action in 1636. The government built a memorial shrine for him in Yongsan mountain in Gyeongju. See the following note for further information.

67) The year of *imjin* returned in 1832, and in the previous *imjin* year, 1592, Suun's ancestor, Choe Chinip, made important contributions to the government, when the Japanese invaded Korea. 1816 was a *byeongja* year, and in another previous *byeongja* year, 1636, Choe Chinip was killed during the Manchu invasion of Korea.

68) Tao Yuan-Ming (陶淵明) of ancient China composed such a poem after returning home from a government position.

69) Yen Tzu-ling (嚴子陵) of the Han dynasty in China declined a high government position when it was offered and lived in a rural village, spending his time fishing.

70) These are geographical descriptions of Gyeongju area, Suun's hometown.

71) Yongchu refers to the waterfall of Yongdam in Gumi Mountain in Gyeongju, where Suun meditated and received his revelation.

72) Maryong is a part of Gumi Mountain.

73) This phrase is based on the Chinese thinker Tao Yuan-Ming's mythical utopia. According to Tao Yuan-Ming's story, fishermen were traveling on a boat and saw peach flowers floating along. They searched and found a beautiful mythical garden of peach trees. Here Suun is comparing the beautiful scene of Yongdam to the peach garden in Tao's story.

74) Chiang T'ai-kung (姜太公) was a famous Chinese statesman during the Chou dynasty. He loved fishing in the water near his home, but eventually became the teacher of the rulers of Chou dynasty in China. Here Suun is comparing the water scene near his home and his father's dream with that of Chiang in ancient China.

75) Chou Tun-i (周敦頤, 1017-1073) of the Sung dynasty in China was a great Confucian scholar, who laid the foundation of Neo-Confucianism. He did not seek a government position but lived a hermit life in a lotus flower garden. He loved the lotus flower and compared it the superior man (*chun-tzu*, 君子). Suun is comparing Chou Tun-i to his father, who also lived near lotus flowers and held a similar world view.

76) Chuke Liang (諸葛亮, 181-234) was a statesman in ancient China during the Three Kingdom Period.

77) The Book of Changes (I Ching) is an important classic in Confucianism which contains cosmological and ethical principles.

78) Suun is stating that his Way and Confucius' Way are similar in respecting Heaven and emphasizing moral virtues, but different in the method of spiritual training.

79) *Gung eul* (弓乙) are symbols of eternity and the Way that Suun realized. *Gung* (弓) is spiral form in vertical way and *eul* (乙) is spiral form in horizontal way.

80) These are the four fundamental virtues in Confucianism.

81) "Keeping the good mind and having the right spiritual force" (*susim jeonggi*, 守心正氣) is one of the most important ideas in Chondogyo. It means keeping the pure and good mind, which is one with the mind of God, and having the right spiritual energy and right conduct.

82) A famous writer in the ancient Chinese Chin dynasty.

83) At this time Donghak had been outlawed by the government and Suun was wanted by the authorities.

84) Written in November 1863.

85) Cheonhwangsi was the first king of China, according to legend.

86) Many people are unable to talk about unknowable and unknown things, but they can say that God is the cause of all things and can affirm the existence and power of God.

87) One implication of these statements is that the phenomena of nature are divine providence. Another implication is that if even non-human creatures know how to fulfill their duties, then human beings should know their creator, God.

88) The things that are difficult to determine are those things in the world which are not clearly explainable. Examples are how and why the Hwang-ha river is

cleansed once every thousand years and a sage appears at that time. Those things which can be explained are called "self evident".

89) When we search for the ultimate and distant origin of all things, especially source of the first parent of humankind, we arrive at the point of the "unknowable," that is, there is no clear and satisfactory answer. Only when we consider God, the creator, as the ultimate cause of all things, does the answer become clear and satisfactory: self evident, true and real.

90) These words were changed by Uiam in the 20th century to "Penitence" because early Donghak believers had celebrations for praying to God. However, these celebrations disappeared in the 20th century.

91) Literally, "in this holy age," which means the new age which arrived with the enlightenment experience of Suun, according to Chondogyo.

92) Master here refers to Suun.

93) This is a prayer or offering to God (Hanullim). It also contains a confession and repentance.

94) Suun had his extraordinary spiritual experience and received the revelation from God on April 5, 1860.

95) This poem was composed by Suun in the spring of 1859, as he was determined to concentrate on his realization of the Way. It was composed at Yongdam, Gyeongju, his hometown.

96) The literal meaning of this poem is "Four Line Quatrain" but the content of the poem is about destiny. The first part of the poem was written in 1860, when Suun received the revelation and the mandate from Heaven. The second part of the poem was written in 1863. The whole poem expresses Suun's feeling of the revelation experience as well as the destiny of Donghak (Chondogyo) which originated in Yongdam in Gyeongju city

97) According to an ancient legend, a sage would be born when the Chinese river Hwangho is purified and when a Chinese phoenix sings.

98) The literal meaning of "the everlasting one" in the text is "the destiny of thousand years"

99) Suun here implies that some of his ancestors were great persons in the history of Korea who contributed significantly to the wellbeing of the nation. Here he expresses his feeling that the great Truth he received from God can save the nation and the world

100) Yongdam is a small place in the mountain where Suun meditated and received his revelation. There is a hut called Yongdam jeong (Yongdam pavilion) on the mountain.

101) Gumi mountain is the mountain where Yongdam is located

102) This poem was composed on New Year's day in 1863

103) The literal translation of the twenty-one letters in the text is the Three (by) Seven Letter (in Chinese characters) which means the twenty-one letters of the Chondogyo incantation.

104) This poem reveals the will and determination of Suun to conquer the evil forces of the world through the spiritual discipline of chanting the incantation

105) This poem was written in April 1863 by Suun as a response to his disciple, Gangsu, who asked about spiritual training. Suun teaches about the important Chondogyo principles of sincerity, reverence, and faith as well as concentrating the mind for the realization of truth

106) Written in 1860

107) This poem reflects the will of Suun, which is compared to the green pine trees.

108) Here Suun and his relationship with his disciples is compared to the crane and its offspring.

109) This poem uses the ancient Chinese idea that the birth of the sage and saints coincides with the appearance of the phoenix and with the renewal of Hwangho River every thousand years. The main idea of this poem is that the old world order is gone and the new age has arrived with Suun.

110) This poem expresses the idea that the wise men rejoice in the arrival of the new age, which is like the spring time when the beautiful flowers are blossoming. It also expresses the process or the search for Truth which is compared to climbing a mountain top step by step and making a joyful sound when one realizes the Truth.

111) This poem encourages us to learn the Truth and to realize the light of the Truth.

112) This is the poem Suun composed about various aspects of nature.

113) This poem expresses Suun's travel to various places.

114) This is in reference to Mencius' saying that when Confucius went up to a great mountain, he realized the smallness of the country.

115) This line of the poem is based on the ancient Chinese scholar Do Yeon Ming's poem.

116) This line of the poem is based on the famous Chinese writer of Sung dynasty, Soh Dong Pa's poem.

117) This line of the poem describes the idea that the great Chinese scholar of the Sung dynasty, Chou Lien Hsi, had a special love for the lotus flower, for it reflected the character of the Confucian superior man.

118) According to legend, there was a reclusive sage in ancient China whom king Yao wanted to make his successor, but when the sage heard this offer, he washed his ears as if he had heard a dirty word. He wanted to remain pure in nature.

119) This line of the poem refers to the legend about the famous Chinese poet of the Tang dynasty who jumped into the water to embrace the bright moon which was reflected in the water.

120) This line of the poem is based on a similar poem composed by Yu Jong Woen, a Chinese poet of the Tang dynasty. It signifies the desolate condition of the world.

121) This line of poem signifies that Donghak (the Eastern Learning) is rising like the sun and that Western Learning (Christianity), which is compared to the western mountain, cannot stop the spread of Donghak

122) The Way here means *Cheondo*, the Heavenly Way.

123) This line of poem emphasizes that if one has a strong and faithful mind, he can experience the deep meaning of the Way, and if one has a firm devotion to God, then all things will work well.

124) Energy here in the text is *gi* (氣). It means inner power or force of mind.

125) When one undertakes spiritual training, it is important to have not only the utmost sincerity and diligence, but also an upright mind.

126) One principle here means the Heavenly Way of Chondogyo.

127) This means that the mind is shapeless, invisible, and immaterial.

128) When the mind is cultivated through spiritual training, then one realizes the virtue or will of God, which is identical with the Way or Truth.

129) The Way or Truth is eternal and is near or within the human heart and human life.

130) This was written in 1863. The title of this poem means words composed in accordance with God's teaching. This poem includes a new determination and hope for the future.

131) The New Year here means 1863.

132) *Ueum* means words composed without planning or contemplation. These words are collections of words composed not in one time but over a period, probably around 1863.

133) The rise of the Southern Cross implies the rise of a new world order. Galaxy may imply a cosmic change.

134) Dust here refers all the evil thoughts and old habits.

135) Cold Food Day refers a special period when people remember their family and relatives.

136) This means the demise of Chin dynasty.

137) This means the rise of Chou dynasty.

138) "The Nine States" here refers to traditional China.

139) A famous lake in China.

140) The famous pavilion beside Dongjeong Lake.

141) This was written by Suun in November 1863. It consists of eight verses. The first part of each verse is conditional, and the second part of it is a response to the first part. This is an important guideline for those who seek spiritual training.

142) The date of composition of these verses is unknown. The Second Eight Verses have conditional parts and some responding parts like the First Eight Verses. But unlike the First Eight Verses, some of the Second Eight Verses end with causes or reasons. These verses are guidelines for spiritual training.

143) Suun received a theme from God. Thus, it is called "Writing on a Theme." It was written in November 1863.

144) This means that harmony and union between humans and God is difficult if one seeks it unnaturally, but if one seeks it like the natural flow of spring time, it is not difficult.

145) This poem is a combination of many different poems. This poem expresses Suun's mind which is concerned about the selfish and chaotic world, and his mind is compared to moon which gives light in the dark world. Also the beauty of nature is expressed in this poem.

146) Vulgar women here is a metaphor for Roman Catholicism. This poem expresses Suun's feeling about himself as a great light for the chaotic world.

147) In the text the Chinese character ten, *sip* (十) looks like the last letter of strong man and soldier, *jeung* (丁).

148) This is a poetic expression relating to a room getting warm when people enter it.

149) This is a poetic expression about the shadow of the mountain in the water as the boat approaches the hillside.

150) The original text combines Korean sounds of the Chinese characters for water, ride, dragon, tiger, tree, etc., but a literal translation of this text is impossible.

151) This poem was composed by Suun in 1864 during his imprisonment in Daegu. It is Suun's last poem. He portrays himself as a lamp without any fault for his imprisonment. Facing his death, Suun expressed here that the Way he founded may look like a dead tree, but has lasting power.

152) This was written by Suun probably in 1863. It is not only about how to write (calligraphy), but also about the spirit of writing and spiritual training and the destiny of the nation.

153) According to the five elements, the tree symbolizes the East (Korea).

154) The literal translation of the transparent and fair rules in the text is "rules without distinction between inside and outside."

155) In Suun's time in the 19th century, Koreans used brush and black ink to write (calligraphy) like in China.

156) This poem portrays the high mountain top and water that flows downward from the mountain top. This natural scene is used as a metaphor for human affairs.

157) The title of this poem indicates that Suun composed it with a sudden realization of the Truth. This poem implies that after a period of painful suffering, a favorable time will arrive for the followers of Donghak/Chondo like the natural phenomenon of the arrival of a flowering spring after a cold and stormy winter.

158) Originally this "Other Poems" was the last part of *Tando Yusimgeub* (The Mind for the Way), but later Chondogyo separated it, in which one can find an encouragement for patience in the process of spiritual training.

159) Also spelled as Tonghak.

160) Chinese here refers to Chinese language called '*Hanmun*' which has been used in Korea for centuries. Korean scholars at the time of Suun during the 19th century knew how to write and read it.

161) Yongdam refers to the place near Suun's home, where he meditated and received the divine revelation.

162) *Hanullim* is the pure Korean term for *Cheonju* (天主), which is the Chinese term, and which is also used by the Roman Catholics for their name for God.

163) *Muwi ihwa* literally means "becoming without action" or "change without action." It can be translated also as "effortless change." A better translation is "natural becoming" or "natural change" or "natural transformation." *Muwi* here is the Korean pronunciation and spelling of the Chinese *wu-wei*, which is a Taoist term, which literally means non-action, but actually means natural life and spontaneous action. It is the way of nature, which is Tao (Dao).

164) *Buryeon Giyeon* is somewhat difficult to translate. It can be translated as "Not so, yet so," "No so obvious, yet obvious," "Not so clear, yet clear," or "Not apparent, yet apparently so." It also means "Not manifest, yet manifest."

165) Suun made such as statement in *Heungbi-ga* (*Song of Comparison*), which is in *Yongdam Yusa* (*Song that Suun left at Yongdam*).

# GLOSSARY

**NB:** *YY* is abbreviation of *Yongdam Yusa (The Songs of Yongdam)*, which is Suun's writing in *han-geul*, Korean script. Unless noted as *YY*, all the writings of Suun herein are from *Donggyeong Daejeon (The Great Scripture of Eastern Learning)*.

*Ansim-ga* (安心歌): *Song of Comfort* in *YY*.

*Boguk anmin* (輔國安民): Supporting the nation and comforting the people.

*Buryeon Giyeon* (不然其然): *Not So, Yet So,* a writing of Suun.

*Cheondo/Chondo* (天道): The Heavenly Way.

*Cheonju* (天主): "Heavenly Lord," God.

**Choe Je-u** (崔濟愚, 1824-1864): Founder of Donghak/Chondogyo.

**Choe Si-hyeong** (崔時亨, 1827-1898): The second leader of Donghak/Chondogyo.

**Chondogyo** (天道教): "The Religion of Heavenly Way," founded by Suun, Choe Je-u.

**Chunam** (春菴): The honorific name of Park In-ho.

***Dodeok-ga*** (道德歌): *Song of Morality* in **YY**.

***Donggwi ilche*** (同歸一體): Returning to the origin and becoming one.

***Donggyeong Daejeon*** (東經大全): *The Great Scripture of Eastern Learning*, which is a main scripture of Donghak/Chondogyo, written in *hanmun*, the Korean version of Chinese.

**Donghak** (東學): "Eastern Learning," which is the original name of Chonodogyo.

***Dosu-sa*** (道修詞): *Poem on Spiritual Training* in **YY**.

***Gangsi*** (降詩): *The Poem I Received from God.* A writing of Suun.

***Gung eul*** (弓乙): The symbols of eternity and the Way that Suun realized. *Gung* (弓) is the spiral form in vertical way and *eul* (乙) is the spiral form in horizontal way.

***Gweonhak-ga*** (勸學歌): *Song of Encouraging Learning* in **YY**.

**Gyeongju** (慶州): The ancient capital city of Silla kingdom, where Suun was born and lived.

***Gyohun-ga*** (教訓歌): *Song of Instruction* in **YY**.

**Haeweol** (海月): The honorific name of Choe Si-hyeong.

**Han-geul** (한글): Korean language.

***Hanmun*** (漢文): Korean version of Chinese.

**Hanullim** (한울님): God in Korean. This is the Chondogyo term for God, and it is identical with Cheonju/Chonju.

***Heungbi-ga*** (興比歌): *Song of Parable* in **YY**.

***Hucheon gaebyeok*** (後天開闢): The recreation of the world.

***In nae cheon*** (人乃天): Man is divine or man is one with God.

***Jigi*** (至氣): The ultimate energy.

***Johwa*** (造化): Making and changing.

***Jumun*** (呪文): *Incantation*.

***Mongjung-noso-mundab-ga*** (夢中老少問答歌): *Song of Dialogue between the Old and Young in Dream* in YY.

***Muwi ihwa*** (無爲而化): Natural becoming, which is based on the Daoist idea of *wu-wei*.

***Nonhak-mun*** (論學文): *A Discussionj on Learning*, a main writing of Suun.

**Park In-ho** (朴寅浩, 1856-1940): The fourth leader of Chondogyo.

***Podeok-mun*** (布德文): *On Propogating Truth*, a main writing of Suun.

***Seonyak*** (仙藥): Mystical medicine.

***Si Cheonju*** (侍天主): Bearing and serving God within me.

***Sinseon*** (神仙): A Daoist idea of mystic sage or immortal.

**Son Byeong-hui** (孫秉熙, 1861-1922): The third leader of Chondogyo.

***Sudeok-mun*** (修德文): *On Cultivating Virtue*, a main writing of Suun.

***Susim jeonggi*** (守心正氣): Keeping the pure mind and having right conduct.

***Suun*** (水雲): The honorific name of Choe Je-u, the founder of Chondogyo.

***Uiam*** (義菴): The honorific name of Son Byeong-hui.

***Yeongbu*** (靈符): Talisman, a mystical sign.

***Yongdam-ga*** (龍潭歌): *Song of Yongdam* in *YY*.

**Yongdam** (龍潭): The name of a spot in Gumi mountain in the city of Gyeongju, where Suun meditated and received revelation.

***Yongdam Yusa*** (龍潭遺詞): *Songs of Yongdam,* a main work of Suun in Korean script.

www.ingramcontent.com/pod-product-compliance
Lightning Source LLC
Chambersburg PA
CBHW021132300426
44113CB00006B/401